THE
HISTORY OF
IRAQ

THE HISTORY OF IRAQ

Courtney Hunt

The Greenwood Histories of the Modern Nations
Frank W. Thackeray and John E. Findling, Series Editors

Greenwood Press
Westport, Connecticut • London

Library of Congress Cataloging-in-Publication Data

Hunt, Courtney.
    The history of Iraq / Courtney Hunt.
        p. cm. — (The Greenwood histories of the modern nations, ISSN 1096–2905)
    Includes bibliographical references and index.
    ISBN 0–313–33414–5
    1. Iraq—History. I. Title. II. Series.
DS77.H86 2005
956.7—dc22   2005020468

British Library Cataloguing in Publication Data is available.

Library of Congress Catalog Card Number: 2005020468
ISBN: 0–313–33414–5
ISSN: 1096–2905

First published in 2005

Greenwood Press, 88 Post Road West, Westport, CT 06881
An imprint of Greenwood Publishing Group, Inc.
www.greenwood.com

Printed in the United States of America

The paper used in this book complies with the
Permanent Paper Standard issued by the National
Information Standards Organization (Z39.48–1984).

10 9 8 7 6 5 4 3 2 1

For my father, who taught me to love history.
For my mother, who taught me to love reading.
For my sister, who taught me to love laughter.
And for my husband, who taught me to love.

Contents

Series Foreword

The *Greenwood Histories of the Modern Nations* series is intended to provide students and interested laypeople with up-to-date, concise, and analytical histories of many of the nations of the contemporary world. Not since the 1960s has there been a systematic attempt to publish a series of national histories, and, as editors, we believe that this series will prove to be a valuable contribution to our understanding of other countries in our increasingly interdependent world.

Over thirty years ago, at the end of the 1960s, the Cold War was an accepted reality of global politics, the process of decolonization was still in progress, the idea of a unified Europe with a single currency was unheard of, the United States was mired in a war in Vietnam, and the economic boom of Asia was still years in the future. Richard Nixon was president of the United States, Mao Tse-tung (not yet Mao Zedong) ruled China, Leonid Brezhnev guided the Soviet Union, and Harold Wilson was prime minister of the United Kingdom. Authoritarian dictators still ruled most of Latin America, the Middle East was reeling in the wake of the Six-Day War, and Shah Reza Pahlavi was at the height of his power in Iran. Clearly, the past thirty years have been witness to a great deal of historical change, and it is to this change that this series is primarily addressed.

With the help of a distinguished advisory board, we have selected nations whose political, economic, and social affairs mark them as among the most important in the waning years of the twentieth century, and for each nation we have found an author who is recognized as a specialist in the history of that nation. These authors have worked most cooperatively with us and with Greenwood Press to produce volumes that reflect current research on their nation and that are interesting and informative to their prospective readers.

The importance of a series such as this cannot be underestimated. As a superpower whose influence is felt all over the world, the United States can claim a "special" relationship with almost every other nation. Yet many Americans know very little about the histories of the nations with which the Untied States relates. How did they get to be the way they are? What kind of political systems have evolved there? What kind of influence do they have in their own region? What are the dominant political, religious, and cultural forces that move their leaders? These and many other questions are answered in the volumes of this series.

The authors who have contributed to this series have written comprehensive histories of their nations, dating back to prehistoric times in some cases. Each of them, however, has devoted a significant portion of the book to events of the last thirty years, because the modern era has contributed the most to contemporary issues that have an impact on U.S. policy. Authors have made an effort to be as up-to-date as possible so that readers can benefit from the most recent scholarship and a narrative that includes very recent events.

In addition to the historical narrative, each volume in this series contains an introductory overview of the country's geography, political institutions, economic structure, and cultural attributes. This is designed to give readers a picture of the nation as it exists in the contemporary world. Each volume also contains additional chapters that add interesting and useful detail to the historical narrative. One chapter is a thorough chronology of important historical events, making it easy for readers to follow the flow of a particular nation's history. Another chapter features biographical sketches of the nation's most important figures in order to humanize some of the individuals who have contributed to the historical development of their nation. Each volume also contains a comprehensive bibliography, so that those readers whose interest has been sparked may find out more about the nation and its history. Finally, there is a carefully prepared topic and person index.

Readers of these volumes will find them fascinating to read and useful in understanding the contemporary world and the nations that comprise it. As series editors, it is our hope that this series will contribute to a heightened sense of global understanding as we embark on a new century.

Frank W. Thackeray and John E. Findling
Indiana University Southeast

Acknowledgments

First, I would like to thank Edward Mickolus, who was kind enough to refer me to his editor, Michael Hermann of Greenwood Press. Words cannot express my gratitude to my wonderful and patient editor, Sarah Colwell of Greenwood Press. Without her this book simply would not have been possible.

My research for this book was greatly assisted by the patient and kind staffs of the Fairfax County Public Library, the Loudoun County Public Library, and the George Mason University library. I thank them all for their boundless assistance with my endless research questions.

Writers are a unique tribe and often band together to support each other. My writing career has been advanced by many such writers' groups. For me, the most influential of these groups is Invisible Ink. I would like to thank each of my fantastic colleagues for their support and encouragement but most especially Robert Kresge, the Founding Father and driving force behind Invisible Ink.

On a more personal note, very special thanks go to the following people for their unwavering support and friendship. Each of you means more to me than you will ever know: Lynn Cary, Vance Hedderal, Hannah Taylor, Sandy Knox, Lisa Glover, Elise Sanford, Danielle Angeline, and Michael Ball. I thank each of you for your support, confidence, and advice.

Several writers' e-mail groups provided additional moral support and encouragement. I also owe considerable gratitude to my faithful accountant and dear friend, North Carolina State Senator Hugh Webster. I thank my friend, Kory Embrey, who kindly provided significant IT advice and assistance during the production of this book.

I owe my family my most profuse thanks for their endless patience with my writing. Writing, by its nature, is a solitary profession that requires long hours toiling away from the company of friends and family. My sister, Meredith Runion and my parents, Paula and Edward Runion, were kind enough to wade through my endless first drafts with critical but kind eyes. I also would like to thank my parents for the sacrifices they made to ensure that I received a quality education. I thank my parents and sister for their love and support and for always believing in me, even when I didn't always believe in myself.

My husband is my muse, my inspiration, my best friend, my soulmate, and my constant support. Without him, this book would simply not have been completed. All I can offer him in return is my copious gratitude and all my love.

Timeline of Historical Events

ca. 8000 B.C.E.	Earliest settlements in Mesopotamia appear
7000 B.C.E.	Jarmo, the first village in Mesopotamia is settled
5900–4000 B.C.E.	Ubaid period
5900 B.C.E.	Eridu is settled
4000–3000 B.C.E.	Uruk period
3500 B.C.E.	Sumerian dominance over Mesopotamia begins
300–2350 B.C.E.	Early Dynastic period
2350–2150 B.C.E.	Akkadian period
2150–2000 B.C.E.	Neo-Sumerian period
2112 B.C.E.	Third dynasty of Ur begins

2004 B.C.E.	Elamites overthrow third dynasty of Ur
2004–1595 B.C.E.	Old Babylonian period
1792–1750 B.C.E.	Hammurabi rules Babylon and eventually Mesopotamia
1595 B.C.E.	The Hittites invade Babylonia, thus ending the first dynasty of Babylon
ca. 1475 B.C.E.	Kassites ascend to power in Babylonia
1415 B.C.E.	Amarna Age begins
1157 B.C.E.	The Elamites overthrow the Kassites and take control of Babylonia
1124 B.C.E.	Nebuchadrezzar I drives the Elamites out of Babylonia
883–792 B.C.E.	Neo-Assyrian period
792–595 B.C.E.	Neo-Babylonian period
745 B.C.E.	Assyrian ruler Tiglath-Pileser II overthrows the Babylonian king, imposing Assyrian rule over Babylon
689 B.C.E.	Assyrians sack Babylon
610 B.C.E.	Assyrian Empire falls
605–562 B.C.E.	Nebuchadrezzar II rules Babylon
555–539 B.C.E.	Nabonidus rules as the final Chaldean king of Babylon
539 B.C.E.	Cyrus Achaemenes, king of Persia, conquers Babylonia, incorporating it into the Persian Empire
539–330 B.C.E.	Mede and Persian occupation
331 B.C.E.	Alexander the Great captures Babylonia
331–129 B.C.E.	Macedonian era
312 B.C.E.	Babylon is absorbed into the Seleucid Empire
129 B.C.E.–234 C.E.	Parthian Kingdom
224–626 C.E.	Sassanid dynasty

570	Prophet Muhammad, the founder of Islam, born
622	Year One of the Islamic calendar
634–637	Muslim conquest of Mesopotamia
661–750	Umayyad dynasty rules Mesopotamia
750–1258	Abbasid dynasty rules Mesopotamia
762	Baghdad built
1258	Hulagu Khan sacks Baghdad
1258–1334	Mongols rule Mesopotamia
1334–1509	Jalairid dynasty and Turkomans control Mesopotamia
1509–1534	Safavid dynasty controls Mesopotamia
1534–1915	Ottomans rule Mesopotamia
1622	Bekr Agha's revolt; Safavids retake Baghdad
1638	Ottoman Empire recaptures Baghdad and controls all of Mesopotamia again
1895	Committee of Union and Progress (CUP) "Young Turks" form as a reform movement
1914–1918	World War I
1920	British given mandate over all Iraq at the Conference of San Remo; borders of modern Iraq created; insurrection of 1920 challenges British authority
1921	Conference of Cairo names Faisal I as first king of Iraq; start of the Hashemite monarchy
1925	Mosul is incorporated into Iraq; Iraqi National Assembly convenes for the first time
1928	Iraq Petroleum Company (IPC) created

1932	Iraq admitted to the League of Nations under the sponsorship of the British; British Mandate over Iraq officially ends
1933	Ghazi I, the second Hashemite monarch, takes the throne
1939	Ghazi I dies in a car accident; his son, Faisal II, takes the throne; as Faisal II is a minor, a regent is appointed
1941	Rashid Ali al-Gailani leads revolt
1943	Iraq joins in World War II against the Axis powers
1945	Iraq becomes a member of the United Nations
1946	Iraq forms the Arab League
1948	Britain and Iraq sign the Portsmouth Treaty, causing the Wathbah Rebellion
1953	First free general direct elections are held in Iraq; Faisal II reaches majority age and takes the throne
1955	Iraq enters Baghdad Pact with Iran, Pakistan, and Turkey
1958	Free Officers overthrow British-backed monarchy
1960	Iraq joins the Organization of Petroleum Exporting Countries (OPEC)
1963	Arif and the Ba'athists assume power
1967	Arab–Israeli War
1968	Ba'athists take control of Iraq; Al-Bakr becomes president
1973	Second Arab–Israeli conflict occurs
1978	Egypt and Israel, with the assistance of the United States, enter the Camp David Accords
1979	Saddam Hussein assumes power in Iraq

1980–1988	Iran–Iraq War
August 2, 1990	Iraq invades Kuwait
January 1991–February 1991	Gulf War I
1991–2003	Iraq endures a decade of UN weapons inspections and economic sanctions
March–April 2003	Gulf War II
December 2003	Saddam is captured outside Tikrit
January 2005	Iraqis, in their first free general election in more than 50 years, elect a National Assembly to develop a constitution and new democratic government

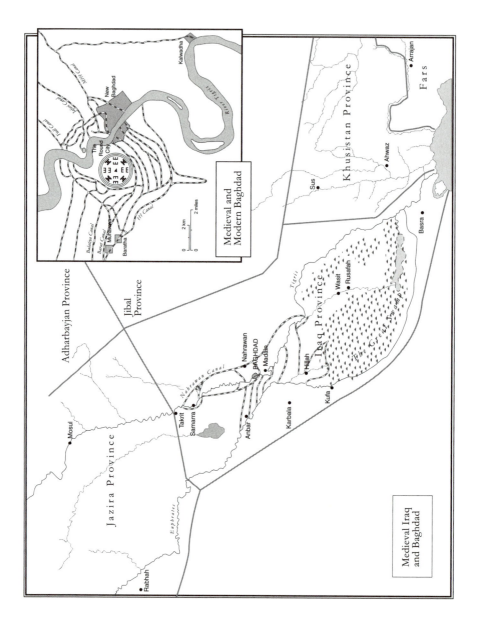

Medieval and
Modern Baghdad

Medieval Iraq
and Baghdad

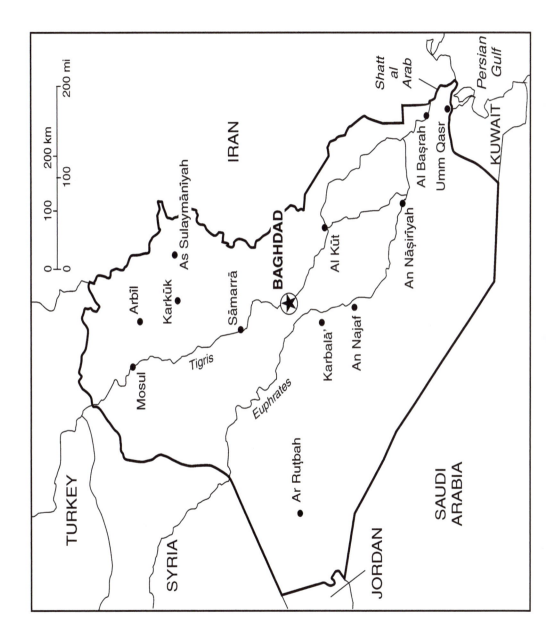

1

The Land and People of Iraq

For many Americans, the Republic of Iraq is a nation seeped in mystery and shadows. In the past 15 years, the United States has fought two wars in Iraq; yet the average American knows very little of the people and the rich history of this fascinating country. For the past two years, Iraq has dominated the nightly news and the foreign policy of the United States and, by extension, the world. Iraq was a mainstay of the most recent American presidential election, and, if the recent Iraqi elections are any example, Iraq is taking its first steps toward a true democracy and may become the first democratic nation in the Middle East. As the future of Iraq is being lived and written right now, a clear understanding of the history of Iraq is crucial in our new global environment.

The current boundaries of Iraq are an artificial creation of the British and French after World War I. Prior to that time, what we now call Iraq was roughly equivalent to Mesopotamia. The term "Mesopotamia" means the land between the rivers and is associated with the cradle of civilization. Indeed, modern-day Iraq was where civilization began. Legends hold that modern-day Iraq is the site of the biblical Garden of Eden. Some 50 miles outside Basra, an ancient tree is allegedly the Tree of Adam and Eve and is a popular tourist site.

This chapter provides an introduction to Iraq, including a brief factual overview of its geography, economy, current political system, social characteristics, and cultural life.

GEOGRAPHY

Iraq is approximately 168,000 square miles, about the same size as California and slightly smaller than Texas. In comparison with Iraq's near neighbors, Iraq is smaller than Iran but larger than Syria. The Tigris and Euphrates rivers flow southeast through Iraq, toward the Persian Gulf, and join at Shatt al-Arab, just north of Basra. The rich banks and tributaries of the two great rivers created a highly fertile, arable plan and set the stage for civilization to develop. The rivers often bring massive flooding, destroying crops and riverside towns. Enormous irrigation systems are required to make much of the land farmable. Additionally, southern Iraq suffers from poor natural drainage that leads to soil oversalinization, a major problem at several points in Iraqi history.

Iraq's richest natural resource is the black gold found beneath the surface: gallons of petroleum that make up more than 95 percent of contemporary Iraq's economy. As of 2000, it is estimated that Iraq contains more than 310 billion barrels of oil reserves, the second-largest reserves in the world.

Iraq's only seacoast is a small 36-mile (58-km) strip of land on the Persian Gulf, so named during the Persians occupation of Mesopotamia starting in 539 B.C.E. Before that, it was commonly called the Chaldean Sea or the Sea of the Rising Sun. Iraq's major ports are Basra, at the confluence of the two rivers, and at Umm Qasr. Iraq's tiny coastline barely provides enough access to export oil, and the ports are relatively shallow. At least part of the Iraqi invasion of Kuwait in 1989 was based on the desire to have access to Kuwait's lucrative seaports.

To the west, Saudi Arabia, Jordan, and Syria border Iraq. Iran sits to the east, and Turkey is to the north. Kuwait is on Iraq's southwestern border on the Persian Gulf. The current borders of the Middle East are the result of a British Mandate in 1920 following World War I.

Iraq is further divided into 18 provinces called *muhafazah*. The provinces of Iraq are Al Anbar, Al Basrah, Al Muthanna, Al Qadisiyah, An-Najaf, Arbil, As Sulaymaniya, At Ta'mim, Babil, Baghdad, Dahuk, Dhi Qar, Diyala, Karbala, Maysan, Ninawa, Salah ad Din, and Wasit. In the north, three provinces make up the semiautonomous Kurdistan region. The Kurds reside mostly along the porous borders with Turkey and Iran in the high, difficult mountain climate and terrain. Baghdad, the capital, sits at the center of the country, on the Tigris River. Other major Iraqi cities include Mosul, Basra, Tikrit, Karbala, and Najaf.

Most of Iraqi land is nonarable and is used as pasture for flocks of sheep and goats. The desert is mostly plains rising into a mountain range along the borders with Turkey and Iran. The rich wetlands of southern Iraq are home to the Marsh Arabs, an ancient people that lived in reed houses and herded water buffalo. Sadly, Saddam Hussein drained these marshes in the 1980s to prevent Iranian and Kurdish soldiers from taking refuge in them and thus destroying the Marsh Arabs' way of life. After the American defeat of Saddam in 2003, much work has been done to revitalize the marshes, but they are only a shadow of the gorgeous ecosystem they once were.

The area along the banks of the Tigris and Euphrates is arable. However, agriculture depends on river water from irrigation systems. Complex irrigation systems dating back to Sumerian times still provide water to the outlying regions. As one can imagine, flooding can be a major concern and destructive, but flood control projects started in the 1950s help mitigate the devastating effects. The main Iraqi crops are dates and cotton, although grains and vegetables are grown in the vast fields near Mosul.

Iraq is located on the historical trade routes connecting East and West. Being at the crux of early civilization gave Iraq access to the wealth, culture, and splendor of the world. Of course, it also made Iraq a valuable conquest. Over the six millennia of recorded history, Iraq was frequently invaded and conquered, leading to the dynamic heritage, rich history, and vibrant cultural tapestry of Iraq today.

The climate of Iraq is mostly dry and hot, although there are marked contrasts in weather as one travels through the country. Southern Iraq enjoys considerably more rainfall than the north, especially during the summer months. In Shatt al-Arab, lush date groves are cultivated. Baghdad, located near the middle of the country, averages summer temperatures of 105°F/40°C and hovers around 40°F/5°C in winter. December to February is the rainy season around Baghdad. In the height of summer, temperatures can soar to highs of 120°F in the capital city. In Mosul, in the northern part of the country, weather extremes are common in the winter and summer. However, Mosul enjoys such fair weather in April and November that it has been dubbed the "City of Two Springs." The mountain regions enjoy mild summers and heavy snow in the winter. Hajj Omran is a favorite ski resort, located near the Iranian border. Heavy mountain snows can lead to spring flooding in the spring in central and southern Iraq.

ECONOMY

The oil industry is at the center of Iraq's economy and accounts for more than 95 percent of Iraq's revenues. Iraq is a member of Organization of Petroleum Exporting Countries (OPEC). The Iraq Petroleum Company was nationalized in 1972 and produces most of the oil in Iraq. The main customers of Iraqi oil are Iraq's Middle East neighbors. The Iran–Iraq War, Gulf War I, and the subsequent United Nations (UN) embargoes severely crippled oil exports. After the UN lifted the embargoes imposed after Gulf War I and prior to Gulf War II, oil exports reached about one-third of the pre-1980 amount. Iraq controls approximately 10 percent of the world's oil reserves.

Although the production and refining of petroleum dominates the Iraq economy, other major Iraqi industries include chemical production, textiles, leather goods, construction materials, and electronics. Agriculture of wheat, barley, dates, rice, vegetables, and cotton provides work for about a third of Iraq's labor force. However, agricultural production is not sufficient to provide food for the entire population, and Iraq must rely on imports to sustain its population. Shepherding of cattle and sheep also makes up a portion of the Iraqi economy.

Ravaged by wars, embargoes, and sanctions, Iraq must rely on significant foreign economic aid. Severely restricted exports and imports have caused significant inflation (estimated at 27.3 percent in 2003). Oil production has not yet reached the level of the late 1970s. As of January 2004, oil production was at 2.2 million barrels per day. Prior to Gulf War II, production stood at 2.8 million barrels per day.

The currency of Iraq is the new dinar, and the coinage is the dirham and fils. The foreign exchange rate has fluctuated wildly during the sanctions and the wars. Stabilizing the currency will be just one of the challenges of the new Iraqi government. As of 2003, the gross domestic product (GDP) of Iraq was approximately $39 billion, but the GDP growth rate was an abysmal –20 percent.

PEOPLE

Iraq is home to approximately 25.5 million people, with a population growth rate of 2.84 percent. The vast majority of Iraqis identify themselves as Arab (75 to 80 percent). The Kurds make up 15 to 20 percent of the population. The remaining 5 percent is comprised of Turkomans, Assyrians, and other ethnic groups.

Tribes, language, and religion divide Iraqi society. Loyalty to family and tribe is a significant factor throughout Middle Eastern society. Although the introduction of the Islamic faith challenged individual loyalty to family tribes, tribalism remains a significant force in Iraqi life, especially in the rural countryside. Urbanization, a centralized government, and education slowly muted the traditional tribal influence, but many Iraqis retain traditional tribal customs.

Additionally, tribal ties often have a great effect on the political mores and structure of Iraq. Most Iraqis feel much greater connection to their family and tribe than to their country. Nationalism in the Western sense of supreme loyalty to the nation does not exist. Some 85 years after the creation of the Iraqi state, Iraqis might identify themselves as Iraqi but only after first identifying their religion and tribal heritage. As Phoebe Marr explains, "Among the legacies of tribalism in Iraq are intense concern with family, clan, and tribe; devotion to personal honor; factionalism; and above all, difficulty in cooperating across kinship lines—the underlying basis of modern civic society."[1]

As for language, most Iraqis speak Arabic, while the Kurds speak Kurdish, creating a language barrier. It is impossible to speak of an Iraqi identity without also discussing the religious sects that constitute Iraq: Arab Shiite Muslims, Arab Sunni Muslims, Kurds, and Christians. Many Kurds are also Sunni Muslims. Religion is one of the primary segmentations of Iraq society, and understanding the significance of these religious differences cannot be understated.

As will be discussed in chapter 4, the Islamic schism between Shiites and Sunnis resulted from a dispute over the selection of caliph, or religious leader, after the death of the Prophet Muhammad.

Briefly, the Shiites hold that only descendants of Muhammad or Ali, son-in-law and cousin of Muhammad, can hold the caliphate. Understandably, direct lineage to Muhammad or Ali has become muddled over the past 1,400 years. Therefore, *mujtahids,* who generally claim some blood relationship to the Prophet or to Ali, oversee the Shiite community. By having one religious leader, the Shiite Muslims have formed a more cohesive community than the more secular Sunnis.

In contrast, Sunnis support any rightly elected caliph as long as the succession laws set out in the Quran are followed. The majority of Muslims around the world are Sunni. Interestingly, this majority is inverted in Iraq. Sunnis are the minority, while most of the Iraqi population is Shiite. In fact, there are three times as many Shiites as Sunnis in Iraq. However, Sunni Muslims have held political power since the time of the Ottomans, and this inevitably leads to Shiite resentment and often oppression. Most of Iraq's Shiite population is centered in southern Iraq.

Unlike the Shiites, the Sunnis do not follow one religious leader. Instead, they follow the customs proscribed by the Prophet, called the Sunna, and the Islamic law, called the sharia. Therefore, the Sunnis do not have as strong a sense of community and connection as the Shiites and tend to be more secular. As a whole, they tend to favor a less religious form of government. Most of the Sunni population is concentrated in northern Iraq, and the Sunnis dominate the cities of Iraq and the urban population in the famous Sunni triangle. The Sunni triangle stretches from the Iranian border to the north of Baghdad to the border with Syria to the west.

The Iraqi Kurds share a cultural, linguistic, and religious identity with Kurdish populations in other countries, especially Turkey and Iran. Most Kurds are Sunni Muslims and probably descended from the ancient Medes, although their true origins are now obscured. Their nationalistic identity is not to Iraq but, rather, to a desired Kurdish nation-state, called Kurdistan by the Kurds themselves. The Kurds who dwell in the semiautonomous Kurdish region in the north of Iraq would prefer separation and independence from the Iraqi nation. During Ottoman rule, there were several Kurdish dynasties that ruled in northern Iraq, but none survived for long. Several times in the past 30 years, Kurds have struggled for independence. However, these movements did not enjoy cohesive backing from the autonomous Kurds and were ultimately unsuccessful.

Rather than Arabic, the Kurds speak a Persian-language derivative called Kurdish, although dialects vary across Iraq. The two main dialects spoken in Iraq are Kurmanji and Sorani, and there are significant cultural and political divisions that accompany each dialect. The Kurds live in the three northernmost provinces of Iraq and traditionally enjoyed a rural, mountainous lifestyle in the Zagros Mountains. However, the Iran–Iraq War and oppression by the government of Saddam Hussein led to an extensive migration of the Kurds. Most have now resettled into cities and towns. Their capital is at Arbil.

Other populations in Iraq include the Turkomans and non-Muslim minorities, including Christians, Jews, Yazidis, and Sabians. The Turkomans are Sunni Muslim descendants of the Seljuk Turks who conquered Iraq in the 1200s. Most Turkomans live in the north, near the Zagros Mountains, and make up approximately 2 percent of the Iraqi population. Although they are proportionally a fraction of the overall population, the Turkomans have been influential in the political history of Iraq and continue to hold prominent positions in the Iraqi government.

As famously commemorated in the Bible, the Jewish population of Iraq arrived as Babylonian slaves in the sixth century B.C.E. However, when Israel was created, the vast majority of the Jewish population, especially in Baghdad, returned to their homeland by 1951.

Three Christian sects call Iraq home and make up 3 percent of the Iraqi population. Chaldeans originated as followers of the theologian Nestorius and are now unified with the Catholic Church. The Nestorian Christians are probably descended from Byzantine slaves. After World War I, the British settled the Assyrians, members of the Nestorian church who did not reunite with the Vatican, in northern Iraq. Integration of the Assyrians has been challenging, as Iraqis, especially the Kurds, have long resented these Christian intruders.

The Yazidis practice a form of Zoroastrianism. They are related to the Kurdish tribes and live near Mosul. Another small minority is the Sabians, who observe a curious and unique blend of Christianity and Islam. The Sabians reside mostly in the south of Iraq near the port city of Basra.

Marsh Arabs, called the Ma'dan, are a mostly Shiite population who dwell in the southern Iraqi marshlands near the confluence of the Tigris and Euphrates rivers. They follow an ancient way of life and have inhabited the marshlands for more than 5,000 years.

Sadly, the building of the Saddam Canal has decimated them, and the population has dropped to less than 40,000 people. During the rebuilding of Iraq after Gulf War II, some water has been returned to the marshland, and the Ma'dan's way of life is being revived.

POLITICAL STRUCTURE

Iraqi political structure is currently in flux. Recent elections created a National Assembly to develop a democratic constitution and method of government. These historic elections—the first free elections in more than 50 years in Iraq—mark a turning point for Iraq, the Middle East, and the world. The entire world can only wait to see if this radical change takes root and flourishes in the sands of Iraq or whether the Sunnis, Shiites, and Kurds will descend into the chaos of a civil war.

On October 3, 1932, Iraq declared independence from the British administration following World War I. Although Iraq was nominally a republic with judicial, legislative, and executive branches, in reality, prior to Gulf War II, dictator Saddam Hussein controlled Iraq with the assistance of regional governors and a National Assembly.

When the Ba'th Party gained power in 1968, the Iraqi constitution was adopted and gave the Revolutionary Command Council (RCC) absolute power. Saddam Hussein chaired the RCC and served as president and prime minister throughout his reign. The National Assembly was comprised of 250 members who served four-year terms. Although the legislature was tasked with approving or rejecting legislation proposed by the RCC, in practice they routinely approved Saddam's legislation. All of Saddam's council of advisers and government leaders were Sunni Muslims like himself.

President Saddam Hussein appointed all judiciary members. The supreme court of Iraq is called the Court of Cassation and is made up of 12 to 15 judges. There are a great many offenses that result in the death penalty in Iraq, and most criminal offenses were harshly punished. There is also a religious court system made up of Christian, Shiite, and Sunni courts that handles personal and divorce cases.

During Saddam Hussein's rule, the only state-recognized political party was the Arab Ba'th Socialist Party. There were several illegal political groups, including the Iraqi Communist Party, the Kurdistan Democratic Party, and the Patriotic Union of Kurdistan.

Additionally, the Shiites have two opposition parties: the Da'wa Islamic Party and the Supreme Assembly of the Islamic Revolution in Iraq.

In 1970, the Kurdish autonomous region was formed and is ruled by an elected legislature. In practical terms, the infighting between the two primary Kurdish political parties has made governance by the Kurdish legislature nearly impossible. Instead, the two parties govern separate shares of Kurdish territory.

It remains to be seen what government the Iraqis will develop for themselves after the recent elections.

NOTE

1. Phebe Marr, *History of Modern Iraq* (Boulder, Colo.: Westview Press, 2004), p. 18.

2

The Cradle of Civilization

Was modern Iraq really the biblical Eden? Some scholars believe that Eden was situated in southern Iraq, between the fertile Tigris and Euphrates rivers. Whether or not Eden actually existed, Mesopotamia was the cradle of civilization. In the fertile crescent of Mesopotamia, writing, mathematics, and the world's first codified legal system began. The Sumerians invented agriculture and irrigation and put the wheel to use in manufacturing pottery and for transportation.

Unfortunately, modern Iraq has suffered such war and strife as to make archaeological excavation difficult to impossible. The hypotheses presented here are what is currently known about the origins of Mesopotamia, but they can and will probably change as archaeologists and historians discover more secrets in the shifting sand dunes of Iraq.

PREHISTORIC IRAQ

Archaeologists have found evidence of humans in Mesopotamia during the Paleolithic Age (25,000–5000 B.C.E.). These humans, like prehistoric mankind the world over, were probably nomadic hunter-gatherers and primitive cave dwellers. In Shanidar, in northern Iraq, there lies a prehistoric cemetery dating back to the Ice Age.

The earliest settlements in Mesopotamia were established between 8000 and 7000 B.C.E. in the floodplain of the Tigris and Euphrates. Although it is difficult to ascertain with certitude, scientists theorize that the environment was less arid in prehistoric times and therefore more conducive to agrarian life. It is possible that the annual river flooding was much more severe than today. Certainly, the Tigris and Euphrates were closer together in ancient times than they are today.

In the late 1940s, Robert Braidwood led a team of archaeologists at Qalat Jarmo in northern Iraq. Braidwood discovered a tiny village that appeared to have been settled around 7000 B.C.E., predating Eridu, the earliest city in the south by more than 1,000 years. Jarmo, because of its location in the hill country, probably received considerable rainfall, which made it environmentally conducive to farming. Additionally, the Jarmo site lay near the now dried riverbed of an ancient stream. Braidwood found evidence of cultivated grain and domesticated animals, supporting his argument that agriculture began at Jarmo.

There were probably many such small villages in northern Mesopotamia between 7000 and 6000 B.C.E. At Tell Hassuna, just south of modern Mosul, archaeologists discovered the first indicators of crude pottery—another sign of a dawning civilization.

The Samarrans, in central Mesopotamia, developed the principles of irrigation. Samarra, a contemporary village to Jarmo, did not receive enough rainfall to allow for cultivation of crops. They created canals and early irrigation troughs to draw on the nearby Tigris River. The Samarrans were also famous for their distinctive pottery, with precise geometric bands and animate figures.

UBAID PERIOD (5900–4000 B.C.E.)

No one is certain of the origins of the people who took the Shinar Plain in southern Mesopotamia. One legend claims they were half man, half fish. It is far more likely, if less colorful, that they were nomadic sheepherders who arrived in Mesopotamia around 5900 B.C.E. and decided to settle along the rich, fertile banks of the Euphrates River. By domesticating wild sheep and goats as well as raising grain such as barley and wheat, the nomads were able to begin farming and creating an agricultural society.

Like the Nile River in Egypt, the fertile banks of the Tigris and Euphrates made agriculture and trade possible, thereby setting the environmental stage for civilization to develop. By 5900 B.C.E., the southern portions of the Tigris and Euphrates were well settled.

From these bustling settlements, the famous ancient cities of Eridu, Ur, and Uruk developed. The ancient city of Ur[1] was about 12 miles to the northeast of Eridu, and Tell al-Ubaid lies some four miles beyond that. Uruk lies some 25 miles to the northwest. These sites are where civilization was born.

Sumerian life was based on mankind's relationship with a vast pantheon of gods. The Sumerians believed that each city-state belonged to its patron deity and that governance of the cities was delegated to a king by the gods. Thus, the temple (and later ziggurats, or stepped temples) became the center of Mesopotamian city life. Sumerians believed that the gods actually resided in their statues and therefore inside the temples at the top of the ziggurats. If raiders removed a god's statue, the town was left godless in the Sumerians' worldview.

The Sumerian creation legend states that the city of Eridu (modern-day Tell Abu Shahrain) was the birthplace of mankind. The tale of the water god Enki and his consort, Ninhursag, found on a cuneiform tablet at Nippur, contains significant links to the biblical creation story of Adam and Eve. For example, both stories focus on a shared rib between male and female humans. It is interesting to note that the great platform temple, a precursor to the ziggurats, at Eridu is dedicated to Enki, who figures so prominently in the Sumerian creation myth, along with Enlil, the god of air and An, the god of the heavens.

The ruins at Eridu lie 12 miles west of the Euphrates, although archaeologists believe that it once perched on the banks of the great river. Pottery shards from the Ubaid period were discovered in the ruins of the temple. Archaeologists unearthed 12 layers of temples at the Eridu site, suggesting that Eridu was indeed begun around 5900 B.C.E.

The people of nearby Tell al-Ubaid created marvelous sage green pottery. Archaeologists and historians specializing in the Near East generally classify prehistoric Mesopotamian sites by ceramic style. Therefore, the distinctive greenish pottery of Tell al-Ubaid came to characterize an entire era of early Mesopotamian life. This distinctive pottery style was found at sites at Ur and Eridu, suggesting that the three cities were contemporary and engaged in trade. Ubaid pottery has been discovered near the northern Iraq city of Mosul, in Syria, and in Saudi Arabia, suggesting that the Ubaid culture spread throughout the Near East.

About 35 miles to the northwest of al-Ubaid and Ur, the town of Uruk (Old Testament Erech) thrived. By 4000 B.C.E., Uruk sprawled over 250 acres—the largest town in the ancient world. The city wall alone is more than five miles long. Uruk thrived because of its location near the Euphrates and its position at the crux of the trade routes between the northern and southern settlements. Eventually, it grew to more than 1,200 acres—much larger than Rome at the height of the Roman Empire.

German archaeologists discovered two great temple complexes at Uruk. Both were early ziggurats, one to the goddess Inanna. The other, the White Temple of Uruk, is the first known temple to sit atop an artificial mountain, which must have supported an imposing ziggurat in its day.

Perhaps the most significant find at Uruk was plain, unadorned pottery. Archaeologists theorize that this utilitarian pottery was the first mass-produced trade item. Mass production of pottery required the world's most significant invention: the potter's wheel. Later, it would be turned vertically and used for transport, further advancing the agrarian economy and culture.

In addition, as agricultural technology advanced, fewer farmers were needed to grow the food that the cities depended on. These advances left room for the growth of specialized labor and professional classes, such as potters, priests, and artisans. Archaeologists also discovered a number of beautifully sculpted pieces, suggesting that skilled labor was available to create them, and a flourishing trade gave them the needed materials, specifically stone. The development of professions led to more people living in the towns, which grew to become cities. Society became increasingly stratified. Urban life focused on religion, and the great ziggurats became the center of everyday life.

Meanwhile, in what is now northern Iraq, several villages existed, though it seems clear that they never reached the size and influence of the southern cities. Ubaid pottery was found at Ninevah, near the modern-day city of Mosul, suggesting trade routes and relationships with the great southern cities. Additionally, so-called Halaf ware from Tell Halaf in modern-day Syria was found, indicating flourishing trade with northern cities. Halaf culture sprung up around 5700 B.C.E., some 200 years later than the southern cities, and probably extended through northern Iraq until it waned around 5000 B.C.E.

URUK PERIOD (4000–3000 B.C.E.)

The origins of the Sumerian people are unknown. Joan Oates, in her excavations at Choga Mami, believes that the northern Samarran culture and the southern Ubaid culture began to mingle around 5000 B.C.E. It is likely that the two cultures combined to produce the world's first empire.

The Sumerians ruled Mesopotamia for more than 1,000 years (3500–2350 B.C.E.). Their empire began at the great city-state of Uruk, hence the name of this historical era. During this time, Sumerian society became increasingly stratified, even including professional bureaucrats and theocrats.

According to Sumerian religious tradition, a city was the property of the resident god. To honor their patron deity, the Sumerians built monumental ziggurats, decorated with artful frescoes and sculpture. Therefore, city life focused on the ziggurats and no doubt supported an enormous religious infrastructure. Eventually, the ziggurats served as the centers of urban religious culture. It is likely that the priests and priestesses of Sumer oversaw vast complexes of bustling activity. The ziggurats were the biggest employers of their day with a large infrastructure support staff to maintain its prominence in Sumerian life.

The center of Sumerian religion was in the city of Nippur, dedicated to the chief Sumerian god, Enlil. The temple of Inanna, Queen of Heaven, was discovered in the ruins of Nippur in the 1950s. But Nippur's true treasures are the thousands of cuneiform tablets discovered there. The translations of these tables teach us much about Sumerian life and society.

By using extensive irrigation canals, the Sumerians brought agriculture to the desert between the Tigris and Euphrates rivers. Unfortunately, this eventually resulted in the oversalinization of the land and made it unfit for cultivation even today. Over time, they developed the plough. They carefully planned and engineered patterns of dams and dikes and developed a reliable calendar, all of which further aided in successful farming.

Their homes were made of mud bricks or woven reeds, much like the Marsh Arabs of today. Little is known about domestic life away from the city centers, as archaeologists have focused on unearthing the monumental ziggurats and their surrounding environs.

Some 300 years before the Egyptians created hieroglyphics, the Sumerians invented cuneiform writing. Using a stylus, the Sumerians made wedge-shaped impressions according to a system of sound based symbols and pictographs. Writing initially developed to support trade by creating permanent records of transactions and inventory. Eventually, however, writing became used for recording poetry, legends and epics, and religious life. By 2700 B.C.E., there were vast libraries in many Sumerian towns.

Another writing-related Sumerian invention was the cylinder seal, which functioned as a signature for property owners and merchants of the day. Generally carved out of stone, the cylinder seal was rolled over wet clay to leave an impression identifying the owner.

Additionally, the Sumerians are credited with creating arithmetic, based on the number 60. We get our 24-hour day and 60-minute hour directly from the Sumerians. The 360-degree circle is based on the Sumerian mathematical system. They also developed square and cubic roots. The Sumerians created a system of weights and measures. The base weight was the mina, which was subdivided into 60 shekels.

The Sumerians also created the first formal school, the *edubba*, to teach cuneiform writing and mathematics. Literally meaning "tablet house," the *edubbas* trained scribes in skills such as accounting, surveying, and early geometry.

Art flourished and produced the epic poems of Gilgamesh and the treasures discovered at the Royal Tombs of Ur. *The Epic of Gilgamesh*, discovered on an original cuneiform tablet at Nippur, tells of King Gilgamesh of Uruk wandering the earth and encountering fable-like adventures in a futile quest to find immortality. This and other Sumerian works are predecessors to the biblical Old Testament stories.

EARLY DYNASTIC PERIOD (3000–2350 B.C.E.)

From Uruk, the Sumerians expanded to create a network of city-states, with their own dynasties and distinct cultures. Each city-state was politically independent and dedicated to its own patron deity.

Not surprisingly, the city-states were often at war with each other over scarce natural resources, especially water. The Early Dynastic period is characterized by perpetual struggles for dominance among the city-states. During this time, standing armies were developed to protect each city-state and frequently battled for conquest and dominance.

Sumerian Kingship

The kings—called *lugals*—were probably originally military leaders during this period of increasing civil strife. Ultimately, the position became hereditary, and thus the world's first dynasties were created. The Sumerian kings ruled with secular authority, as evidenced by the first known royal palace at Kish in northern Iraq. However, they were entrusted to rule by the patron deity to which the city was dedicated. As such, the king played the part of the god Dumuzi and engaged in the sacred marriage rites at the opening of the New Year.

The famed British archaeologist Leonard Woolley excavated the ancient city of Ur in the 1920s. His most famous discovery was the Royal Tombs of Ur, which dated to Sumerian times. There were 1,850 graves on the site, both royal and commoner alike. The offerings of food and drink contained in the commoner graves indicate that the Sumerians believed in an afterlife.

Although Woolley found 16 royal tombs at Ur, only two were spared from looters. In the intact tombs, Woolley found elaborate death pits—evidence that the court was sacrificed and buried with the monarch in the Early Dynastic period. The courtiers were dressed in intricate costumes and carrying riches thought to be needed in the afterlife. Woolley and others believed that this indicated that royalty might have been considered divinity during the Early Dynastic period.

The Sumerian King List gives the names of Sumerian rulers and is probably more fictional than fact. However, it also served the purpose of promoting the divine right of kings to rule their territory—and anything else they could gain. Kish was the first city-state to unite most of Sumer. Uruk, under the kingship of Gilgamesh, seized control from Kish. Control of Sumer shifted between various dynasties throughout the Early Dynastic period. King Eannatum of Lagash obtained control of the city-states of Kish, Uruk, Ur, and Mari and expanded his territory into Iran around 2500 B.C.E.

To pay for the constant war and necessary tributes, the citizens of Sumer were heavily taxed until about 2400 B.C.E., when King Urukagina ascended to the throne. He instituted a series of reforms designed to protect individual rights. Urukagina's reforms set the stage for Hammurabi to develop the world's first legal code.

However, Urukagina's reforms were not to last. Lugalzaggesi, king of Umma, deposed him. He was able to unite most of the city-states under one rule. However, Sargon of Akkad, who created the world's first empire, overthrew him.

AKKADIAN PERIOD (2350–2150 B.C.E.)

The Sumerian's wealthy, thriving, and constantly quarreling towns soon proved to be tempting for hordes of invaders intent on conquest. Sargon was the leader of the warlike tribes of the Semitic Akkad based in northern Mesopotamia. According to the legend, Sargon was the son of a priestess. She placed him in a basket of reeds and set the basket on the gently lapping waves of the Euphrates. Sargon was rescued by a gardener and raised as his son. Sargon means "True King" and was probably a title assumed to give the commoner legitimacy to rule. Sargon rose to power in Kish during Lugalzaggesi of Uruk's rampages. He united the previously independent Mesopotamian city-states under one ruler and ruled from his northern capital of Agade. Although the Sumerians managed to regain control of Ur from the Akkadians around 2100 B.C.E., the rule of Sargon I marks the end of cultural dominance by the Sumerians.

Tales of Sargon's conquest of the Sumerians were found on a clay tablet at Nippur. Sargon defeated the lugals of Uruk, Ur, Umma, and Lagash and forcibly integrated them into his empire. They were ruled by an Akkadian governor and overseen by Sargon from his capital at Agade in the north. The location of Agade has yet to be discovered by archaeologists. Sargon cleverly claimed his right to rule from the religious traditions of Sumer and Akkadia. Sargon commanded an enormous army of more than 5,400 men.

Over time, Sargon's rule stretched as far as Lebanon, Turkey, Iran, and Syria. He reigned for more than 55 years and united the Sumerians and the Akkadians into one extensive kingdom, setting the stage for later Babylonia. Sargon founded the first Mesopotamian dynasty, which lasted until 2108 B.C.E.

Realism in art was one of the most important advances of the Akkadians. This was probably part of the effort to deify the king,

Naram-Sin. This deification of the king represented a significant shift from the Sumerian belief that the gods delegated authority to the king. Naram-Sin is usually depicted in artwork wearing the horned helmet of a god, indicating that he was considered actual divinity rather than just a earthly representative of a divinity. Unlike his grandfather, Sargon, Naram-Sin declared himself a god. This presumption was considered sacrilege among the Sumerians, and the Curse of Agade tells the tale of Naram-Sin's divine comeuppance.

Sargon's descendants spent most of their time trying to reconquer restless city-states. His grandson, Naram-Sin, enjoyed a long 36-year reign and increased his empire to the north and east. Naram-Sin's son, Sharkalisharri, was the final king of Sargon's line. His empire fell under the invasion of the Guti, a people from the Zagros Mountains of Iran.

NEO-SUMERIAN PERIOD (2150–2000 B.C.E.)

The Guti reign lasted about 100 years, and, as they ruled from afar, it is unlikely that they held much sway over Sumerians or Akkadian daily life. For example, Lugel Gudea of Lagash began reconstruction around 2140 B.C.E., indicating that he—and his city-state—retained their independence from foreign rulers. In 2120 B.C.E., Utuhegal, the king of Uruk, overthrew the Gutian overlords.

In 2112 B.C.E., Ur-Nammu ushered in the third dynasty of Ur. A divine king and a tightly organized bureaucracy characterize this dynasty. Ur-Nammu followed Gudea's example and began large-scale reconstruction projects. He built the great ziggurat at Ur—a temple to Nanna, the moon god. He also refined the legal codes governing Sumerians and developed the principle of legal compensation. His legal code outlines specific monetary compensation to be paid for various acts.

Ur-Nammu ruled for 18 years and was followed by his son, Shugli. Over time, the Euphrates River shifted to the west, leaving the once-thriving cities stranded in the arid desert. For example, the ancient site of the city of Uruk is now more than 12 miles from the Euphrates.

The third dynasty of Ur ended with the reign of the final Sumerian king, Ibbi-Sin. Cities were suffering being so far away from the banks of the river, causing food shortages, and famine prevailed. The Elamites, from Khuzistan in modern Iran, overthrew the third dynasty of Ur around 2000 B.C.E.

In 2004 B.C.E., the Elamites took the city, and the great culture of Sumer was left to be rediscovered and reenergized by the Babylonians.

NOTE

1. It may interest students to know that Max Mallowan and his famous author spouse Agatha Christie are generally credited with excavating Ur.

3

Babylonia

For the next 2,000 years, Mesopotamia was a melting pot, under almost constant assault and governed by competing empires. The city of Babylon rose to prominence as the Assyrians and Babylonians jockeyed for power. After the fall of the Assyrian Empire in 610 B.C.E., Egypt became the chief rival of Mesopotamia. Mesopotamia transformed from a network of loosely linked city-states to a unified, centralized nation-state. Additionally, Mesopotamia endured many conquests during this time, including those by the Medes, the Persians, the Macedonians, the Parthian Kingdom, and the Sassanid dynasty.

OLD BABYLONIAN PERIOD (2004–1595 B.C.E.)

After the Amorite kings obtained control of Mesopotamia, they worked to unite the independent Mesopotamian city-states under their rule. Although the city of Babylon was born during the Early Dynastic period, it was a cultural backwater until 1895 B.C.E., when the Amorites founded their first dynasty there. Although the temple of Marduk was built during the Ur III period, it is unlikely that Babylon was an early religious center because it was not until the second Amorite king, Sumulael, commissioned elaborate thrones for Marduk and his goddess wife that Marduk began to achieve prominence in the Babylonian pantheon of gods. "The much later tale, that Sargon committed sacrilege by carrying holy soil from Babylon for the founding of Agade ... was clearly invented to give substance to Babylon's subsequent claims to sanctity."[1]

When Hammurabi ascended to power, prestige, and prominence, Babylon was a minor city-state, jostling for power among the other Mesopotamian city-states. Hammurabi (1792–1750 B.C.E.) made Babylon the center of a thriving empire, not unlike the preceding Sumerian civilization. During the early years of Hammurabi's reign, the most powerful Mesopotamian ruler was Shamshi-Adad (1813–1781 B.C.E.), who ruled Assyria in southern Mesopotamia. However, Shamshi-Adad's sons were not as able rulers, and after his death, Assyria's dominance decreased, setting the stage for Babylonia's rise. Instead of conquering other city-states and empire building, Hammurabi focused on building Babylon and ordering Babylonian society. Babylon was situated in the heartland of the country and therefore was vulnerable to attack from all sides. Hammurabi's internal focus and wise alliances with the Assyrians and the Sumerians gave Babylon the safety and security to grow and to flourish.

By the thirtieth year of his dominion over Babylon, Hammurabi's interests turned to empire building. Hammurabi successfully attacked Larsa and therefore ruled over central and southern Mesopotamia. He followed up this victory by seizing Mari, which lay northwest of Babylon in modern-day Syria. Eventually, Hammurabi conquered the Assyrian stronghold of Eshunna. Therefore, Hammurabi controlled all of Mesopotamia from his seat in Babylon, and the area then became known as Babylonia. Although later rulers lost significant portions of Hammurabi's controlled territory, Babylon maintained dominance over Mesopotamia for the next 1,000 years, and the seat of power shifted permanently to the north.

Hammurabi is best known for his legal code published in the thirty-ninth year of his reign, which encompassed civil, criminal, and commercial law and became the basis for modern law. It is not a true legal code because it is not all encompassing but rather a sampling of legal tenets in an "if-then" series of statements. For example, "If a man has accused another man and has brought a charge of murder against him, but has not proved it, then his accuser shall be put to death." There is no indication that these statements were the basis for legal disputes to be resolved but were more akin to moral commandments. However, the *misharum,* or edicts, were oral proclamations that did carry the force of law and were based on Hammurabi's code. Hammurabi granted more rights and freedoms to women in Babylonia than did most ancient societies. Women and slaves were allowed to have their own property and money. Slaves were allowed to earn wages elsewhere after their duties to their masters were completed and even to eventually purchase their freedom.

By making Marduk the chief divinity of the Babylon Empire, Hammurabi created the first monotheistic state. Marduk inspired the Enuma Elish, the creation tale that may have in turn inspired the writers of the Old Testament Genesis. Marduk was the main divinity honored in the Babylonian New Year festival. In this key rite, the ruling monarch would "take the hand of Marduk" in a symbolic marriage and thus receive a confirmation of kingship by the god Marduk that was viewed as essential to legitimate rule by the Babylonians. The statues of the gods, which the Babylonians believed to contain the spirits of the deities themselves, were carried through the streets in a long, celebratory procession, and the creation epic Enuma Elish, in which Marduk possessed a starring role, was read aloud.

While he did "take the hand of Marduk" in the New Year festivities, Hammurabi was a secular ruler, an important distinction from earlier rulers who declared themselves divinity. His law code makes several references to the king being a steward or shepherd overseeing the population on behalf of the gods. Judicial power and administration, therefore, were transferred from the temple and priesthood to the kings.

Social stratification was based almost solely on economic standing in Babylonian society. Hammurabi's legal code calls out three social classes: *awilum,* meaning freeman; *mushkenum,* meaning royal dependent and certainly inferior to the *awilum;* and *wardum,* meaning slave. Note the absence of a warrior class or a priesthood caste. There was a popular assembly, most probably made up of landowners or heads of households administered by a council of advisers. Any male citizen could participate in an assembly, so it is likely that the landowners or other prominent citizens made up the council.

The population was mostly urban based, although there were small clusters of rural settlements. These settlements appear to have been based on land grants and holdings that were kinship based. Therefore, much of Babylonian and Mesopotamian land was owned privately, although the temple and the king were major landholders as well.

Hammurabi's son, Samsu-iluna (1749–1712 B.C.E.), did not prove to be as adept a ruler as his father. He quickly lost control of the south to revolt. The south set up the Sealand dynasty and tried to revive the glories of ancient Sumer. Additionally, the Sealand dynasty controlled access to the Chaldean Sea, the southern date palm plantations, and the wildlife-rich marshes. In time, Babylonia shrunk to just the city and a relatively small area of surrounding countryside. Yet its influence continued for the next 2,000 years.

In 1595 B.C.E., the first dynasty of Babylon ended when Murshili I led the Hittites from Anatolia in Asia Minor and sacked Babylon. Samsu-ditna, the final Amorite king of Babylon, lost the throne to the Hittites. It is probable that Murshili I allied with the Kassites, a people settled north of Babylon, as the Kassites were the only Middle Eastern people not to suffer Hittite conquest. The Hittites stole the statue of Marduk from the temple, which, to the Babylonians, meant the city was now godless. The time between the Amorite dynasty and the Kassites is shrouded in mystery. Either the historical record ceases entirely as the scribes struggled for subsistence under their new rulers or the missing cuneiform tablets remain undiscovered and undeciphered. In either case, little is known and much is guessed at. Most historians believe that the Sealand king, Gulkishar, took the opportunity to swoop in and capture the throne of Babylon.

The Kassites

By returning the statue of Marduk that had earlier been plundered by the Hittites (and thus, to the Babylonian mind-set, restored the god himself to the city), the Kassites ascended to power around 1475 B.C.E. The origins of the Kassites are unclear. The Kassites likely came from the mountains in the east and founded a state around the east Tigris during the reign of Samsu-iluna.

Eventually, they were able to wrest control of the south from the Sealand dynasty. The Kassites governed a unified Babylon for more than 500 years, considerably longer than any other Mesopotamian dynasty. However, few specifics are known about their rule. The secrets lie in undiscovered cities beneath the desert dunes or in untranslated cuneiform tablets.

The Kassites did not rule from Babylon; instead, Babylon was relegated to the religious capital of Mesopotamia. Their capital was at Aqar Quf, the site where the Tigris and Euphrates flow closest together, slightly to the west of modern-day Baghdad. In a significant departure from the Old Babylonian period, the Kassites ruled over a united nation that was akin to the size and scope of Hammurabi's rule rather than the politically fractious city-states of old. However, much like the later Romans, the Kassites allowed the local customs and laws to prevail. They allowed Babylonian traditions, religion, and customs and were themselves eventually absorbed into Mesopotamian society.

The Kassites also rebuilt many sacred sites in the ancient Sumerian cities of Ur, Eridu, and Uruk, which no doubt endeared them to the locals. Kassite societal structure was roughly akin to the much later British feudal system. Tenants held and worked the land and paid the landholders with the bounty they were able to produce. Taxes were high to support vast infrastructure projects, rebuilding initiatives, and a well-organized military.

By 1460 B.C.E., the Kassites conquered the southern Sealand city-state and unified all of Babylonia under their rule. For the most part, the Kassites were not interested in aggressive conquering of lands but instead preferred to defend their borders. This represents a crucial departure from earlier, land-hungry rulers. By 1415 B.C.E., during the reign of Kara-indash, the Kassites established diplomatic relations with Egypt, ushering in the Amarna Age, so called because of the discoveries of cuneiform tablets documenting this period in Amarna, Egypt. Babylon's fortuitous position along the trade routes to Egypt brought great prominence and wealth to the city. Eventually, the Babylonian and Egyptian dynasties even intermarried.

During the Amarna Age, Assyria rose again to power by conquering the Hurrians of western Syria. Eventually, the Assyrians also intermarried with the Kassite dynasties. However, Babylonians were unwilling to accept an Assyrian king's rule and assassinated Kara-hardash, the son of a Babylonian king, and an Assyrian royal daughter in a local revolt. Assyria then placed another Kassite king, Kurigalzu, on the Babylonian throne. He captured the Elamite capital of Susa.

Around 1297 B.C.E., the Kassites aligned with the Hittites, at least partly in response to the rising power of Assyria. Indeed, the heightening of the conflict with Assyria was one of the hallmarks of the Kassite rule of Babylon. The Assyrian monarch, Tukulit-Ninurta I (1244–1197 B.C.E.), was intent on expanding Assyria's empire and, perhaps even more important, winning control over the trade routes. After taking the Babylonian king Kashtiliash IV to Ashur as a captive, Tukulit-Ninurta I ruled over Babylon for 32 years. After Tukulit-Ninurta I's death, the Babylonians, under Adad-shuma-usur (1216–1187 B.C.E.), were able to drive the Assyrians out of Babylon.

However, the Assyrians had to struggle to maintain control over Babylonia as they frequently clashed with the revitalized Elamites. In order to weaken the Assyrian Empire, the Elamites invaded Babylon and raided the surrounding towns. Finally, around 1157 B.C.E., the Elamites, led by Shutruk-Nahhunte I, marched into Babylon. They carried off the enormous monument of Hammurabi's legal code and the statue of the Babylonian god Marduk. In 1155, the last Kassite ruler of Babylon, Enlil-nadin-ahhe, was killed by the Elamites.

Nebuchadrezzar I (1126–1105 B.C.E.), of the southern Mesopotamian city of Isin, brought glory back to Babylon by taking the Elamite capital, thus avenging the earlier Elamite sack of Babylon and returning the statue of Marduk to the city. Nebuchadrezzar's I's younger brother, Marduk-nadi-ahhe, challenged Assyria by attacking the city of Ekallate. The Assyrian's brutally retaliated, and the destruction brought famine to Babylon. Legends state that the Babylonians even turned to cannibalism to survive. For the next two centuries, Babylon suffered from internal political instability with multiple tribal leaders vying for power.

About this time, the nomadic Aramaean tribes became a serious threat to Babylon and Assyria. Although it is unclear why the Aramaean tribes left their homeland, this influx of people was a drain on the cities and resources of Babylonia. The Aramaeans may even have raided and ransacked the Mesopotamian cities. There was at least one Aramaean king of Babylon, Adad-apla-iddina (1069–1048 B.C.E.). However, the most lasting legacy of the Aramaeans was that Aramaic became the language of the land until the Muslim conquest.

After the fall of the Isin dynasty, the second Sealand dynasty (1026–1006 B.C.E.) rose to power in the south. Simbar-Sipak ruled for 18 years before power shifted again to the House of Bazi (1005–986 B.C.E.) from the Tigris region.

Dynasty E, consisting of some five Babylonian kings, ruled Babylon during the ninth century B.C.E. Although Assyria was the dominant power of the time, the militaristic Assyrians were focused external conquest and thus struck an uneasy peace with Babylon. The ruling dynasties of Babylon and Assyria intermarried, and there was a lengthy period of relative peace.

The reign of Assurnasirpal II (883–859 B.C.E.) was the beginning of the Neo-Assyrian Empire. However, Assurnasirpal II did not interfere with his Babylonian counterpart, Nabu-apla-iddina. Therefore, Babylon enjoyed a prosperous renaissance age during which art, culture, and literature flourished. Toward the end of Nabu-apla-iddina's rule, he entered into a treaty with Assurnasirpal's son and successor, Shalmaneser III. Shalmaneser III's son, Shamshi-Adad, called on the treaty for Babylonian help in defeating an internal rebellion. The Babylonians honored the treaty; however, after the rebellion was quieted, they renegotiated the treaty with Shamshi-Adad. The new treaty was a humiliation to Shamshi-Adad, who quickly conquered Babylon and carried off two kings. He then christened himself "King of Sumer and Akkad."

It is significant to note that, after Shamshi-Adad's death, his regent was his wife, Sammu-ramat (Semiramis). She ruled as monarch for a five full years and clearly held all the power of kingship. Mesopotamian women enjoyed much greater freedom and prestige than they did in most ancient societies.

The Assyrians unquenchable thirst for conquest created an empire that was so large as to be nearly impossible for them to effectively rule. They were continuously fighting to quell revolts and rebellions in their conquered territory, depleting their military strength and power.

Adad-nirari III (810–783 B.C.E.), in an attempt to solve the chronic tribal unrest throughout Babylon, agreed to honor the Babylonian religious ceremonies and traditions as long as Assyria was able to dictate control over all political affairs in Babylonia. To the Babylonians, however, the Assyrians were the oppressors, and this gave the southern-based Chaldeans an opportunity to take the Babylonian throne.

NEO-BABYLONIAN EMPIRE (792–595 B.C.E.)

The Chaldeans were a tribal people from the swamps of the lower Euphrates valley. They are first recorded in the ninth century B.C.E.

and paid rich tribute to Babylon and Assyria for several centuries. Their location along the well-frequented southern trade routes gave them unique items to send as tribute. From the time of Nebonassar, intricate and detailed historical records were kept. Scholars attribute this to the rise in interest in astronomy. One of the current meanings of the word "Chaldean" is astronomer.

It is possible that the Chaldeans descended from the Sealand dynasties of the south. When a Assyrian coup occurred after the death of Adad-nirari III, Eriba-Marduk ascended to the Babylonian throne around 770 B.C.E., ushering in the Neo-Babylonian period. Eriba-Marduk is credited with rousting the Aramaeans from Babylon.

In Assyria, Tiglath-Pileser III (744–727 B.C.E.) ascended to the throne. Under Tiglath-Pileser, Assyria once again became the dominant power. In 729 B.C.E., Tiglath-Pileser again brought Babylon under Assyrian control by "taking the hand of Marduk" in the New Year's festival. Babylonia was to remain under Assyrian control until 626 B.C.E. despite the best efforts of the Chaldean-led Babylonians.

Merodach-Baladan took control of the Babylonian throne and wisely proffered vast tributes to the Assyrian king. In turn, the Assyrian ruler allowed Merodach-Baladan to control Babylonia. This second kingship, which really equated more closely to a governor, was employed several times throughout the long period of Assyrian dominance. As long as the Babylonian king did not threaten Assyrian territory and continued to supply exotic tributes, the Assyrians allowed the Babylonian king to reign and Babylonian customs and culture to continue.

Merodach-Baladan was able to loosely unite the Chaldean tribes into an anti-Assyrian group. However, Merodach-Baladan did not count on the ascension to the Assyrian throne of Sargon (literally, "true king"). After conquering much of the ancient world, Sargon once again took Babylon in 710 B.C.E. After Sargon's death in 705 B.C.E., the deposed Merodach-Baladan again wrested control of Babylon from Sargon's son, Sennacherib, in 703 B.C.E. Sennacherib again took control of the Chaldean tribes and installed his own son on the throne in 699 B.C.E.

In 694 B.C.E., the Elamites took control of Babylon in response to an Assyrian raid on their capital. After the Assyrians imprisoned the Elamite king, Mushezib-Marduk, supported by the Aramaeans, took the throne. Together with the Elamites, Mushezib-Marduk marched on Assyria and defeated them at Halule.

In response to this aggression, Assyria destroyed Babylon in 689 B.C.E., doing significant damage to the sites of Entemenanki and Egalish. Sennacherib installed his son, Esarhaddon, as overseer in Babylon. Eight years later, Sennacherib fell victim to patricide, and Esarhaddon worked to reconcile Babylon and Assyria. To that end, he worked to rebuild the elaborate city his father had destroyed. Eventually, Esarhaddon was able to conquer Egypt but not before creating a two-pronged line of succession. Two of his sons would rule, one over Assyria and the other, his equal, over Babylonia.

When Esarhaddon fell during one of his aggressive territorial campaigns, the dual monarchy came into effect. In practice, Assurbanipal, the Assyrian monarch, wielded considerably more power than the weaker Babylonian monarch, Shamash-shuma-ukin. In 652 B.C.E., revolt broke out, and civil war lasted for four years. In the end, the Babylonians resorted to cannibalism again, and Shamash-Shuma-ukin committed suicide by throwing himself into the flames of his burning palace. Although Assurbanipal set up a fictitious Babylonian kingship, Babylon and Assyria were again united under his rule until 627 B.C.E. Less than 20 years later, the Assyrian and Babylonian empire of the Kassites had crumbled. However, Assurbanipal's most enduring legacy is that of the vast cuneiform library at Ninevah. Without these precious cuneiform documents, we would not have the understanding or the knowledge that we have today about the ancient world of Babylon.

However, the Assyrians were fond of building grand palaces, monuments, and temples that were understandably easier for archaeologists to discover. For this reason, Assyrian history dominates this period. Babylonian culture melded with Assyrian military and political might and absorbed their conquerors, creating a true melting pot.

In 625 B.C.E., Nabopolassar, a Chaldean, wrested control of Babylon from Assyria. After several failed attempts to conquer Assyria, Nabopolassar was aided by the Medes attack on the Assyrian capital of Assur in 614 B.C.E. Although he arrived after the city fell, he and the Median king, Cyaxares, drew up a formal treaty, ratified by the marriage of their descendants, Babylonian Crown Prince Nebuchadrezzar and Amytis, daughter of Cyaxares. Although there were some minor skirmishes over the next few years, by 610 B.C.E. the Assyrian Empire had fallen.

In 605 B.C.E., Nebuchadrezzar inherited the Babylonian throne from his father, Nabopolassar, thus ushering in the most glorious reign in Babylonian history. Nebuchadrezzar is familiar to most modern readers as the king who took vast numbers of Jews hostage and looted treasures from the Temple of Solomon. During Nebuchadrezzar's time, Egypt replaced Assyria as Babylon's most potent enemy. Most of Nebuchadrezzar's reign was occupied with combating Egypt and navigating through the constantly shifting political alliances of the smaller, satellite countries around Babylon and Egypt. At the great battle of Carchemish, an Egyptian garrison city in Syria, Nebuchadrezzar, then still the crown prince, attacked and drove the Egyptians from Syria. Several years later, a great battle between the Egyptians and Babylonians occurred in the southern Egyptian city of Migdol (Magdolus). Although the battle itself was probably a draw, from this point until the end of the Neo-Babylonian dynasty, Egypt was confined mostly to its borders.

As a consequence of defeating Egypt, Babylon now demanded tribute and the riches of conquest from Egypt's prior vassals, including Judaea. For a few years after the battle of Carchemish, Jehoiakim, king of Judaea, paid tribute to Babylonia. However, after the indecisive battle of Migdol, Jehoiakim unwisely stopped paying tribute, perhaps believing that the Migdol battle would result in the Egyptians rising to power again. Jehoiakim's gamble proved to be foolhardy and brought about the fall of Jerusalem in 597 B.C.E. As described in the Second Book of Kings,

> The king of Egypt did not march out from his own country again, because the king of Babylon had taken all his territory, from the Wadi of Egypt to the Euphrates River.... At that time the officers of Nebuchadnezzar king of Babylon advanced on Jerusalem and laid siege to it and Nebuchadnezzar himself came up to the city while his officers were besieging it. Jehoiachin king of Judah, his mother, his attendants, his nobles and his officials all surrendered to him.... As the Lord had declared, Nebuchadnezzar removed all the treasures from the temple of the Lord and from the royal palace and took away all the gold articles that Solomon king of Israel had made for the temple of the Lord. He carried into exile all Jerusalem: all the officers and fighting men, and all the craftsmen and artisans—a total of ten thousand. Only the poorest people of the land were left.... He [Nebuchadrezzar] made Mataniah, Jehoiachin's uncle, king in his place and changed his name to Zedekiah. (2 Kings 24:7, 10–12, 13–14, 17)

However, the true "Babylonian Captivity" of the Jews occurred nine years later, when Judaea again failed to pay its promised tribute. Nebuchadrezzar sacked Jerusalem after a long siege. According to the agreement struck when Nebuchadrezzar placed Zedekiah on the Judaean throne, each of Zedekiah's sons was put to death in front of him and his eyes burnt out. As for Jerusalem, again we look to the Second Book of Kings:

> He set fire to the temple of the Lord, the royal palace and all the houses of Jerusalem. Every important building he burned down. The whole Babylonian army, under the commander of the imperial guard, broke down the walls around Jerusalem. Neburzaradan the commander of the guard carried into exile the people who remained in the city, along with the rest of the populace and those who had gone over to the king of Babylon.... So Judeah went into captivity, away from her land. (2 Kings 25:9–11, 21)

The Jews would not return to their homeland for 70 years. Although Nebuchadrezzar did not clash directly with the Medes and was able to maintain his alliance with them during his lifetime, he built the famous Median wall north of Babylon as a defense against northern aggression and created a double city wall that encircled Babylon.

He also restored much of Babylon, especially the famous Ishtar gate that stood more than 23 meters high. He created the famous Hanging Gardens of Babylon, most probably as decoration for his southern palace and to please his Median wife, Amytis. This was a series of earth-covered terraces planted with exotic trees, flowers, and shrubbery. All told, the Hanging Gardens of Babylon were estimated to be 75 feet high and were truly a wondrous oasis in the middle of the desert. They were one of the Wonders of the Ancient World. Finishing his father's work, Nebuchadrezzar placed the highest shrine on Etemenanki. Etemenanki was situated near Esagila and was a vast ziggurat that had been rebuilt many times in Babylonian history. After Nebuchadrezzar's death in 562 B.C.E., he was succeeded by his son and then by a Babylonian general. In 555 B.C.E., Nabonidus took the throne.

Nabonidus was an aging Babylonian general, descended from a priestess of the Assyrian moon god Sin. The Assyrians had established a small seat at the city Harran. Nabonidus was concerned mostly with restoring the ancient customs and shrines of Sumer and Akkad and especially his mother's temple. Nabonidus's devotion to the Assyrian god Sin did not sit well with the Babylonians, who remained devoted to Marduk. Despite negotiating peace between the Lydians (in Asia Minor) and the Medes in 585 B.C.E., he was never able to revive the alliance with the Medes that Nebuchadrezzar enjoyed, and therefore, after Nebuchadrezzar's death, the Babylonian accord with the Medes disintegrated. Additionally, he inexplicably left Babylon on a 10-year sojourn to Taima, possibly on a missionary drive to for the moon god Sin. Nabonidus was nearly 70 when he returned to Babylon and now faced the greatest threat the Babylonian Empire had yet known: Cyrus Achaemenes of Persia.

MEDE AND PERSIAN OCCUPATION (539–330 B.C.E.)

The Persians were probably descendants of the Elamites. They intermarried with the Median royal line and Cyrus Achaemenes, the king of the Persians and the Medes. One persistent legend is that his grandfather, the Median king Astyages, dreamt that that Cyrus was destined to rule over all Asia. Astyages ordered the newborn murdered, but a faithful palace servant gave the child to a shepherd to raise. Eventually, Astyages relented and allowed Cyrus to become his servant or page. Cyrus responded by promptly leading a revolt in 550 B.C.E. and was himself then crowned king of Medes. In 539 B.C.E., Cyrus Achemedides led his victorious army into Babylon. The elder king Nabonidus had fled the city, and the Babylonians did not resist Cyrus's attacks. Cyrus wisely left the civil and religious traditions of the Babylonians alone and simply appointed a Persian overseer, called a satrap.

The Persians then established their own dynasty in Babylon, and unlike the preceding foreign dynasties, the Persian kings never assimilated into Mesopotamian culture. Instead, outside influences began to alter the Mesopotamian way of life. For example, cuneiform was replaced with the Aramaic alphabet. In perhaps his most famous act, Cyrus Achemedides freed the captive Jews.

Cambyses II (529–522 B.C.E.) inherited the Persian throne from his father, Cyrus Achemedides, and incorporated Egypt into the Persian kingdom. Although there were several revolts in Babylon, Cambyses II and his successor, Darius (521–486 B.C.E.), managed to organize the kingdom, create a legal system, and undertake massive road construction projects, including building a new capital and digging canals. Darius installed his son Xerxes as crown prince in Babylon, and when Darius died, Xerxes (485–465 B.C.E.) was recognized as the Babylonian king.

However, the Babylonians soon tired of supporting Xerxes' aggressive territorial campaigns, and rebellion broke out. Xerxes recaptured the city in 482 B.C.E. and melted down the statue of Marduk. The city was incorporated into the Assyrian kingdom and taxed very heavily. After Xerxes was assassinated (possibly by the infuriated Babylonians) in 465 B.C.E., his son Artaxerxes (464–424 B.C.E.) was much more lenient with the recalcitrant Babylon. The city was restored to relative peace, although they continued to be forced to pay heavy taxes and tribute.

In 331 B.C.E., Darius III (335–331 B.C.E.) was defeated by Alexander the Great of Macedonia, and Babylon passed to Macedonian rule.

MACEDONIAN ERA (331–129 B.C.E.)

In 331 B.C.E., Alexander the Great captured Babylon and was greeted with gratitude by the Babylonians. Alexander restored Marduk's temple and also restored Marduk to his position as chief deity. He made the city his eastern capital and began restoring the devastation the Persians had wrought. In an attempt to solidify his empire and create a union of the Mediterranean and Middle Eastern people, Alexander the Great married 14,000 Macedonians to 14,000 Babylonian women in a mass ceremony.

Alexander held a massive funeral in Babylon for his dear friend Hephaestion. A portion of the city wall had to be removed for the funeral pyre, and the remains of this massive, charred funeral bier were later found among the temple rubble and outer wall. Alexander died in Babylon in June 323 B.C.E. His successors split into two empires, and by 312 B.C.E., Babylon was absorbed into the Seleucid Empire.

Seleucos or Nicator (meaning "Victorious") founded the Seleucid dynasty (312–249 B.C.E.). Seleucos moved his capital to Seleucia, just south of Baghdad, on the Tigris River. A necessary consequence of this shift in capitals was that Babylon lost most of its former prestige. Although Babylon was never restored to its former glory, Mesopotamia, under the Seleucid dynasty, again became part of a great empire.

Antiochus I (281–261 B.C.E.) decreed that the civilian population of Babylon move to Seleucia. The temple of Marduk was rebuilt and thus established Babylon as a religious center. Additionally, a Greek colony was established in Babylon.

PARTHIAN KINGDOM (129 B.C.E.–234 C.E.)

By 161 B.C.E., the Parthians were well established in Iran and often sparred with the Seleucians for control of Babylon and Mesopotamia. As the Seleucid dynasty fell, Mithradates II, leader of the Parthians, took control of Babylon and Mesopotamia in 122 B.C.E. Most archaeologists believe that Babylon was in ruins by that time, although there is some evidence that religious festivals were still held there. "A text of 93 BC reveals that at least parts of Esagila were at that late time still used for religious services."[2]

Around 75 C.E., the Parthians established their capital, Ctesiphon, opposite Selecuia across the Tigris River. Although Rome attacked Mesopotamia several times, it was not able to wrest control from the Parthians until 64 B.C.E.

Sassanid Dynasty (224–636 C.E.)

After killing the final Parthian emperor, Artaban, the Persian prince Ardachir took Ctesiphon and founded the Sassanid dynasty. Shapur I, son of Ardachir, declared Mazdeism the official religion. Shapur II (310–379 C.E.) repelled the Romans from Ctesiphon.

The empire expanded steadily under Chosroes I (531–579 C.E.) and Chosroes II (590–628 C.E.). In 614 C.E., Chosroes II captured Jerusalem and, according to legend, is said to have carried off Christ's cross. In memory of this stunning victory, Chosroes erected an enormous 100-foot-high arch at Ctesiphon that still stands today.

When the Prophet Muhammad summoned Chosroes II to convert to Islam, Chosros II refused and instead ordered Muhammad captured. In turn, Chosros II's rash action introduced the Muslim conquest of Mesopotamia.

NOTES

1. Joan Oates, *Babylon* (London: Thames and Hudson, 1979), p. 61.
2. Ibid., p. 142.

4

The Muslim Conquest

In approximately 633, the Muslim army, via conquest, introduced the Muslim faith to Mesopotamia. In all of Iraq's vast history, the Islamic conquest holds the most powerful influence and historic significance. Arabic became the prevalent language of the Mesopotamia and Islamic culture, and religion molds the Iraqi self-identity. In this chapter, we survey nearly 1,000 years of Iraq's history as control swung among multiple and competing Islamic dynasties. During this era, Baghdad was built and quickly became the center of civilization in Mesopotamia. After centuries of shifting power and endless battles, the Muslim conquest led to a renaissance of learning and culture.

The Muslim invaders were Arabs, who originated from north of Iraq, in the Arabian Peninsula. Even today, Arabs are the majority population in Iraq. Understanding the significance of this conquest requires understanding the origins and principles of the Islamic faith, and so we begin with a brief overview.

A BRIEF HISTORY OF ISLAM

Arab culture was organized into tribes who answered to a sheik (*shaykh*). The tribes were further divided into specific families and clans. In the sixth century, Mecca, in present-day Saudi Arabia, was a boomtown on the lucrative East–West trade route. Muhammad, the founder of Islam, was born in Mecca in 570 to a young noble widow. After the death of his mother and grandfather, Muhammad was taken in by his poverty-struck uncle, who taught Muhammad to be a shepherd. Over time, Muhammad married and had four daughters.

Perhaps because of his solitary occupation tending the flocks, Muhammad spent considerable time reflecting on the meaning of life and would often retreat into the mountains to think. In his favorite cave, he was visited by the angel Gabriel and given the first verses of the Quran around 610. The Quran is the Islamic religious text and is believed to contain the final and authoritative word of Allah. It also tells the stories of all Muhammad's religious visions and revelations. Gabriel also gave Muhammad the task of calling people to Allah and his service.

Islam was revolutionary because it introduced the concept of monotheism, an afterlife, and a Day of Judgment to the Arab world. The five pillars of Islam are belief in one God and that Muhammad was his Prophet, daily prayers, charity toward the poor, observance of Ramadan, and a once-in-a-lifetime pilgrimage to Mecca. Ramadan is a monthlong observation of the period when the Quran was revealed to Muhammad. During Ramadan, Muslims must fast from sunup to sundown. It also upset the tribal order by claiming that the tie of Islam was stronger than the bonds of familial life. Most Meccans were unreceptive to the new religion and eventually drove the Muslims out of Mecca and imprisoned them in a nearby steep-walled valley. This migration is referred to as the Hegira and is considered the first Muslim community.

In 622, Muhammad took his followers to Yathrib, later called Medina, meaning "the Prophet's city," where he build the first great mosque and created the first Islamic state. Muhammad is credited with writing the first Medina city charter and further developed the Quran and refined Islamic religious principles there. The year 622 is also significant as the first year of the Islamic calendar.

In 624, the Muslims fought three great battles with the Meccans. At the first, the Battle of Badr, the Meccans, acting on the excuse that they wanted to protect a large and valuable caravan along the trade route, marched with more than 1,000 men on Medina. They paused at the small roadside oasis of Badr, believing that the trade caravan was likely to stop there. Muhammad and his small force of 313 men reached Badr first and stopped up the water supply, always a critical resource in the desert. Despite being vastly outnumbered, the Muslims were able to force the retreat of the Meccans and won a splendid victory.

The Muslims were not so fortunate at the Battle of Uhud. Abandoned by 300 hypocrites (those who proclaimed to be Muslim but secretly undercut it), the Muslims faced 3,000 Meccans with only 700 troops. Although it appeared the Muslims would triumph, the foolhardy Muslim archers abandoned their posts, thus allowing the Meccan cavalry to attack from the rear and defeat the Muslims.

The Jewish tribes in Medina signed peace treaties with the Muslims, but eventually, each tribe broke the treaty and engaged the Muslims in battle. The Banu Qaynuqa and Banu Nadir tribes were defeated by the Muslims and forced from the city. The third tribe, Banu Quraiza, coexisted peacefully with the Muslims. The Banu Nadir tribe returned to Mecca and encouraged the Meccans to defeat Islam permanently. The Meccans and their allies assembled a force of 10,000 and marched again on Medina. In desperation, the Muslims dug a wide, deep trench around the city, and the battle became known as the Battle of the Ditch. Despite their best efforts, the Meccans could not breach the trench. Eventually, the coalition collapsed from within and quit the siege.

In 625, Muhammad led a group of 1,400 pilgrims to Mecca for the observance of religious rites at the Meccan shrine of Kabba. While in Mecca on pilgrimage, the Meccans and the Muslims were able to agree to a 10-year period of peace in the Treaty of Hudaibiyah. However, shortly thereafter, one of the Meccan allies attacked and slaughtered a large number of Muslims. In response, Muhammad assembled a force of more than 10,000 men and marched on Mecca. They arrived under cover of night and lit many campfires on the hillsides to make their vast numbers appear even greater. The Meccans surrendered, and Muhammad led a victory march through the city of his birth. He granted clemency to all the Meccans and destroyed the statues of the Arab gods. After making several more pilgrimages to Mecca, Muhammad retired to Medina, the capital of Muslim power. He died in Medina on June 8, 632 when he was 63 years old. His grave is still venerated under the green dome of the Prophet's Mosque in Medina, and his birthplace in Mecca is the site of many Muslim pilgrimages each year.

Muhammad's death lead to a succession problem. According to the Quran, Muhammad was a prophet or messenger in the tradition of spiritual leaders who had gone before. During Muhammad's lifetime, Islamic government was a participative affair including rights for non-Muslims and participative town counsel meetings called *shuras*. After the Prophet's death, Muhammad's followers elected their caliph (*khalifa*), or political and religious leader, who was accountable to a representative council. The first four leaders were called the "Rightly Guided Caliphs" because they followed the system of Islamic government set down in the Quran.

Abu Bakr, the father-in-law of Muhammad, was the first elected successor and was so pious that he earned the nickname "al-Siddiq," meaning "the believer." Umar, who introduced the Muslim faith to Iraq and Persia, followed Abu Bakr. He was assassinated in 644, supposedly by a Christian slave while Umar was praying in a mosque. Uthman, of the clan Umayya, ruled from 644 to 656 and was killed by rebels from Kufa in Iraq. The rebels felt that Uthman ruled unfairly and was vulnerable to fiscal and moral corruption. The uprising was the start of the first Islamic civil war, which is important to understand because many of the prominent present-day Islamic sects arose from this conflict.

As discussed previously, after the Prophet Muhammad's death, the caliphate succession was troubled by internal strife and the challenges of governing a far-flung empire. Muawiya, governor of Syria and a member of Uthman's Umayya tribe, challenged Muhammad's elected successor, his son-in-law, Ali ibn Abi Talib. Some of Ali's more pious supporters broke away and formed the Kharijite sect. Ali fought a great battle against the Kharijites at Nahrawan in Iraq, a slaughter that still reverberates through the Muslim world today. It was a disgruntled Kharijite who assassinated Ali in 661, thus allowing Muawiya to establish his own Umayyad dynasty. Less than 30 years after Muhammad's passing, Islamic leadership became a hereditary monarchy.

The impact of the two early civil wars created divisions that still exist in Islam today. Those loyal to Ali founded the Shiites (Shi'a) sect of Islam, who believe that the caliph must be a member of Ali's or Muhammad's family and is therefore hereditary. The Umayyads believe that the caliph should be elected from the community of

Islamic believers. The Kharijites believe that true piety is the most important qualification in a ruler. The Sunni sect of Islam essentially rejects the beliefs of the Shiites and the Kharijites based on an extension of the Umayyads' succession beliefs.

THE MUSLIM CONQUEST OF IRAQ

As discussed in chapter 3, Chosroes II rebuffed the Prophet Muhammad's invitation to convert to Islam. At this time, the major religions in Mesopotamia were Christianity, Judaism, and Zoroastrianism. During the birth of the Islamic faith, Mesopotamia remained under Persian control. After Muhammad's death, the Muslim army, led by Khalid Ibn al-Walid (meaning "Sword of Islam"), attacked Mesopotamia in 634 and defeated the ruling Persians in the Battle of the Chains. The battle earned this sobriquet because the Persian troops were chained together to prevent desertion. Aided by the Christian Arabs in Hira and other cities, Khalid and his massive army racked up an impressive series of victories. Perhaps this assistance can be attributed to the fact that the Muslims allowed the conquered people to continue their religious practices as long as they paid tribute taxes to the Muslims. However, over time, many conquered peoples converted to Islam, partially based on such factors as lower taxes for Muslims, social acceptance, and the appeal of a monotheistic belief system. In 637, the Muslim army, led by Saad al-Waqqas, took the city of Ctesiphon, thus wresting control of Mesopotamia from the Persians.

The Umayyad Dynasty (661–750)

After Ali's death, Hassan, Ali's son and the grandson of Muhammad, declared himself Caliph in 661. Because of his status as Ali's son, Hassan enjoyed considerable popular support in Mesopotamia. However, Muawiya, the governor of Syria, also announced his claim to the caliphate. To prevent a protracted civil war, Hassan retracted his claim. Muawiya, ruling from Damascus, Syria, became caliph over the entire Muslim world and ruled until his death in 680, thus founding the first Islamic dynasty, the Umayyads.

Muawiya broke with tradition and the succession rules set down in the Quran by naming his son, Yazid, as his successor, thus launching the Second Islamic Civil War (680–692), which, once again, was based on differing interpretations of the succession rules set down in the Quran. Yazid was not a popular choice among many pious Muslims and was directly opposed by his uncle, Ali's other son, and the grandson of the Prophet Muhammad, Hussain (al-Husayn). Hussain set up an opposing government at Kufa, where most of his Shiite supporters lived. At Karbala, Yazid's Syrian army crushed Hussain's opposition. To this day, Shiite Muslims commemorate Hussain's defeat at Karbala and even consider him a martyr. Abd Allah ibn al-Zubayr also established an opposing caliphate from Mecca but was eventually subdued by the Umayyads.

The Syrian Umayyad were a despotic leadership and quelled revolts ruthlessly. Yussaf al-Hajjaj, the Syrian governor of Mesopotamia from 694 to 714, went so far as to purge the Quran of any reference that could be interpreted as encouragement to overthrow the dominant Syrians. He built the new city of Wasit on the Tigris, near Kufa in southern Mesopotamia.

Umar ibn Abdul Aziz was dubbed "the Second Umar" during his rule from 717 to 719 and was considered a just and fair ruler. The Umayyads also were able to expand the Muslim Empire through western Europe into Spain and east into central Asia. The Umayyads did much to establish the written history and traditions of Islam. They also attained great accomplishments in architecture. They built the famous Dome of the Rock in Jerusalem, over the remains of Solomon's temple, to commemorate Muhammad's night journey to heaven as well as the Umayyad mosque in Damascus, with outer walls encrusted with massive, glittering mosaics.

In general, however, the Mesopotamian people despised the harsh, tyrannical Umayyads. In addition, under the Umayyads, many non-Arab converts to Islam were treated as subclass citizens to Arab-born Muslims and were required to pay harsh non-Muslim taxes. In 750, Abu al-Abbas al-Saffah, a descendant of Muhammad's uncle, led the rebellion against the Syrians, thus setting the stage for the second Muslim dynasty, the Abbasids.

The Abbasid Dynasty (750–1258)

The Abbasid dynasty ruled the Muslim world for more than five centuries, including during the Mongol invasion. The Abbasids presided over enormous progress in arts, culture, science, and literature. The city of Baghdad was founded under their rule and was declared their capital rather than the former capital at Damascus. At Khorassan, Abu al-Abbas led the army to a crushing victory against the Syrians and marched on Kufa. In September 749, Abu al-Abbas took Kufa and then established his seat at al-Anbar on the Euphrates River. The Abbasids considered themselves the avengers of Ali and his descendants and thus, in their worldview, claimed more legitimacy to the caliphate than the unpopular Umayyads. They also created a theocracy rather than the more secular government favored by the Umayyads. They treated Arab-born Muslims and non-Arab Muslims as equal. Al-Abbas proclaimed himself caliph and earned the nickname "Bloodthirsty" by ordering the murder of all the members of the Umayyad dynasty.

Only Prince Abdurahman Ibn Muawiya was spared the fate of the Umayyads and escaped to Spain. Prince Abdurahman Ibn Muawiya was elected the emir of Cordoba in 756 and established his own Islamic dynasty there. This Spanish dynasty ruled for more than three centuries and created a rich, vibrant Islamic culture and tradition in Spain. The most lasting achievements of this parallel dynasty were the building of the great mosque at Cordoba and the foundation of the famous colleges of Andalusia. Eventually, the Spanish dynasty devolved into a series of small, competing city-states and was defeated by the advances of the Christian armies from northern Spain.

Although the Abbasid caliphs lost control of other far-flung lands, Mesopotamia remained the heart of Islamic civilization. Abu al-Abbas died in 754, and Abu Muslim installed his brother, Abu Jaffar, as head of the caliphate. Abu Jaffar, in turn, promptly ordered the execution of his brother. Abu Jaffar ruled under the name al-Mansur (meaning "Victorious"). His most famous accomplishment was building the new city of Baghdad (meaning "Gift of God") on the banks of the Tigris River in 762. Although there is evidence that a settlement and small village were located at the Baghdad site from antiquity, al-Mansur created a sumptuous city. He nicknamed it Madinat al-Salam, meaning "the City of Peace." Legend claims that Baghdad was situated on the site of the Garden of Eden, though scholars have found no historical evidence for this claim. Baghdad was dubbed "the jewel of the world" and laid out like the spokes of a wheel with the palace in the center. Al-Mansur's palace was magnificent and was made up of stones from the ruins at Ctesiphon. Because of the enormous gilded front doors, it was dubbed "the Golden Gate." By 775, al-Mansur built a second great palace in Baghdad called Qasr al-Khuld, meaning "the Castle of Eternity." It was destroyed during the Mongol sieges of the twelfth century.

Baghdad was cannily located along the major trade route between the Persian Gulf and China, which no doubt contributed to the city's wealth and enormous population, even larger than Constantinople. It was here that great progress was made in arts, literature, science, and medicine. Baghdad was the center of the Islamic renaissance, and it was here that the three great cultures of the world intersected: Arab, Hellenic, and Persian.

Although the ascension of the Abbasids did not end the debate over the caliphate succession, the Abbasid caliphs enjoyed a lengthy reign. The Alids, as the family of the Prophet, still claimed that Islamic rule was their blood right, and this tension still exists today. Some Abbasid caliphs sought to include the Alids as advisers and counselors; other caliphs believed the Alids were trying to usurp the power of the Abbasids and spent much time trying to stamp them out. Perhaps this explains some significant governmental changes that occurred during the Abbasids' early rule. They eliminated the councils of advisers that were traditional in the Arab world and created a true monarchy.

They wielded the power of life and death over their subjects and were the final religious authority. The vizier (*wazir*) was the chief adviser to the Abbasid caliphs and oversaw a vast bureaucratic administration. By the mid-800s, the Abbasids oversaw a large professional military.

Harun al-Rashid (786–809), who was famously referred to in the story collection of *The Thousand and One Nights,* succeeded Abu Jaffar's successor, al-Mehdi, in 786 after al-Rashid's mother cleared the path to the throne by having her eldest son murdered. The royal intrigues continued when al-Rashid's wife, Zubayda, convinced him to murder his best friend and sentence his best friend's father, the vizier Yahia of Barcemide, to a prison for atheists.

Al-Rashid defeated the Byzantines and was able to tax the Eastern Roman Empire. Although he coped with a hostile dynasty seated in Morocco and the remaining Umayyads from their base in Spain, al-Rashid was a popular leader, and his reign marks the beginning of Baghdad's golden age. Baghdad was the center of civilization for the Arab peoples of the Middle East.

Advances in science were a hallmark of the Abbasid Muslims, especially in the areas of algebra and geometry. The arts, especially poetry, flourished. Wealth poured into the capital from trade with far-flung lands. The great poet Abu Nawas wrote during this time. Scholarship of all types flourished. Harun al-Rashid was especially interested in theological research and founded many of the great schools of Islam. Harun himself made no fewer than nine pilgrimages to Mecca.

Additionally, non-Muslims, called *dhimmis*, were free from prosecution and able to enjoy all the economic and intellectual wealth that Baghdad and the Abbasid Empire had to offer.

Harun was succeeded by al-Ma'moun the Great (813–833). Al-Ma'moun created a House of Wisdom with a vast library. For his time, he was a free thinker and even supported questioning the Quran's precepts. Al-Ma'moun was a wily politician, however, and declared Ali, Muhammad's son-in-law, "the Greatest Companion after the Prophet." As the Shiites believed Ali to be the true heir to the caliphate, al-Ma'moun's veneration of Ali was politically necessary and ensured him the support of the Shiites.

Al-Ma'moun's brother, al-Mu'tassim, succeeded him to the caliphate in 833. Al-Mu'tassim's rule was marked by strife. The people of Baghdad loathed the Turkish "Mamluks" who influenced al-Mu'tassim's rule. The Mamluks were non-Arab slaves from central Asia. However, over time and under the rule of al-Mu'tassim, the Mamluks were able to assume actual political control and reduced al-Mu'tassim and the caliphate to essentially a religious figurehead. Al-Mu'tassim moved his capital to Samara, but neither he nor his successors were able to escape the Turks.

By the 940s, the Abbasids were powerless puppets of the Turks. The Turks consolidated their authority and declared themselves "emir of emirs." The vizier and caliph were stripped of their secular power and retained control only over religious matters. The empire began to crumble as the outlying provincial governors chafed under the ruling Turks' yoke. In addition, much of Iraq's arable land suffered from overcultivation, and the wealth-generating, financial base of Baghdad began to shrink.

The Buwayhids (945–1055)

Fed up with Turkish rule and influence, Ahmed Buwayhid (Buyid) of Shiite-controlled Persia (modern-day Iran) and his brothers seized Baghdad. At first, they were given honorary titles by the ruling Abbasid caliph, al-Mustaqfi. Within 40 days of taking the city, they tossed al-Mustaqfi into prison and installed his young son on the throne. The Buwayhids ruled through their young puppet caliph and, in essence, reduced the caliphate to a political figurehead with some religious authority. Additionally, the Shiite Buwayhids allowed the celebration of Shiite holidays and encouraged the flowering of Shiite disciplines.

During the Buwayhid's rule, their territory was severed into appanages governed by various members of the Buwayhid clan, thus creating constant competition for dominance throughout the Buywahid holdings. Additionally, the Buwayhids were not able to maintain central control over the rebellious countryside. Most of the major cities founded their own ruling dynasties, and the Buwayhids often granted vast tracts of land to those who served loyally in the military. The Buwayhids also were forced to handle the large Turkish army that was garrisoned at Baghdad.

The Ayyarun bandits thrived during this fractured rule and, much like the American Mafia, mastered Baghdad. By the middle of the tenth century, as central Abbasid rule crumbled, there were multiple dynasties throughout the Islamic world. Each of these dynasties developed its own court based on the Baghdad model. Eventually, Baghdad was no longer the center of the Islamic world and learning but, instead, just another Islamic community in the Arab world. In the eleventh century, Fatimid-controlled Cairo, Egypt, assumed its place as the cultural and political center of the Islamic world, a position still enjoyed by Cairo today.

The Seljuk Turks (1055–1258)

The Turkomons, Turkish-speaking Islamic tribes from central Asia, began migrating into the Buwayhid-held lands in the 1040s. General Tughrul Beg (Toghril), leader of the Sunni Seljuk Turks based in Khurasan and commander of the Turkomon armies, took Baghdad in 1055, thus including Iraq in the great Seljuk domains. He murdered the Buwayhid protector of the Abbasidian caliph and took over as puppeteer to the ruling caliph. Tughrul Beg proclaimed himself sultan of the Middle East and North Africa. He broke his secret alliance with the last Abbasid caliph and intermarried with the Abbasid dynasty.

Tughrul Beg went on to conquer Persia. His nephew, Alp Arslan, succeeded him in 1063. His vizier, Nizam al-Moulk, founded the Nidhamiya, the most prestigious Islamic school (madrassa) of the time. Unfortunately, he was assassinated in 1092.

In 1118, the Abbasids again attempted to retake the caliphate. Caliph al-Mukhatadi was killed in the attempt. His brother al-Muqtafi

(1136–1169) was able to free Hilla, Wasit, and Basra. Finally, in 1186, al-Nasir and the Abbasids were able to rid Mesopotamia of the Seljuk Turks, who had been severely weakened by the long crusades and their overextended, far-flung empire.

In 1234, Al-Mustansir founded the Mustansiriya, a madrassa that still operates on the Tigris River in Baghdad, although it was bombed during Gulf War II. In Abbasid times, this ancient university contained many wonders, such as a clock that told the position of the moon and sun at each hour. For many centuries, the Mustansiriya was the foremost madrassa for scholarship of the Quran in the Islamic world. Al-Mustansir and his son, al-Mu'tassim, were not able to defend their empire from the Tatars and, later, the Mongols. Al-Mu'tassim was the last of the Abbasid caliphs.

THE MONGOLIAN INVASION (1258–1334)

By the early twelfth century, the Mongols, led by famed warlord Genghis Khan, dominated all of Asia and were poised to take the Middle East. The great-grandson of Genghis Khan, Hulagu, attacked and sacked Baghdad in 1258. The vizier assisted Hulagu in the hopes that the Mongols would name a descendant of Ali as caliph.

Al-Mu'tassim, the last Abbasid caliph, was strangled and his family murdered during the Mongolian siege of Baghdad. Legend says that it took the Mongols 40 days to execute the entire population of Baghdad. Although the Mongolians wrought devastation on the city's population, they refrained from total destruction of the city itself. However, the Mongols did destroy the great mosque, the Imam Mussa al-Khadim's sanctuary, and the House of Wisdom. Under the Mongols, the practice of Islam was forbidden. The rule of the Mongols was the first time that the Islamic world was under the dominion of a non-Islamic ruler. Sadly, the Mongols also ruined the ancient Sumerian irrigation systems, choking entire regions of Mesopotamia. The destruction of Baghdad created a power vacuum, and over time, the center of Islamic life returned to Cairo.

Hulugu appointed a Mongolian governor and allowed al-Alkami to remain vizier. Hulugu himself ruled from the city of Tabriz in Persia. Hulugu's son rebuilt much of Baghdad and stabilized the country. In 1282, Takudar Khan was named caliph and converted to Islam. Sultan Ghazan built a new system of irrigation canals between the Euphrates and Karbala. When Ghazan died in 1304, several rebel factions competed for power in Iraq.

The Jalairid Dynasty and the Turkomans (1334–1509)

General Hassan Burzug al-Jalairi founded the Jalairid dynasty in 1334, probably because he aligned with the Mongols and allowed their continued sovereignty over Mesopotamia. His son, Awais, went on to add Azerbaijan to the Jalairid Empire.

But the most menacing threat to Iraq in the time of the Jalairid dynasty was the Turkomans. The Black Sheep tribe from Anatolia to the north of Mesopotamia attacked Mosul in 1374. The Turkoman prince, Timer the Lame (or "Tamerlane"), supposedly also a Sunni Muslim, captured and destroyed Tikrit and Mosul. When he learned that the Sultan Hassan had returned to Baghdad, Tamerlane took the city in 1401. Legend says that in response to Tamerlane's order to behead two people each, the Turkomans built 120 pyramids of 90,000 heads.

The so-called Black Sheep dynasty founded by Tamerlane lasted from 1401 to 1467. In 1466, Jihan of the Black Sheep dynasty attacked the White Sheep dynasty, led by Hassan Beg Tawil. The Black Sheep dynasty and the White Sheep dynasty were ancestral enemies. Hassan Beg Tawil was victorious and ruled from the Persian city of Tabriz. The White Sheep dynasty ruled from 1467 to 1509. After a lengthy battle for succession, Hassan Beg Tawil's son Murad Beg took the throne in 1499. After a crushing defeat by a Safavid of Persia, he lost the territory of Azerbaijan in 1503 and then began ruling from Baghdad. On Murad Beg's death in 1509, the White Sheep dynasty ended.

The descendants of the Black Sheep and White Sheep tribes still live in Kirkuk and Tell Afar. The next ruling dynasty allied with the Ottoman Empire, and thus Mesopotamia passed to the control of the Ottomans for nearly 400 years.

5

The Ottoman Empire

The Ottomans conquered Baghdad in 1534 and ruled Mesopotamia until World War I. However, Ottoman control did not extend to the Mesopotamian countryside, which was ruled by native tribesman. After repelling an attack by the Safavids of Persia, Mesopotamia became known as the Province of Baghdad. The 1908 revolution of the Young Turks brought a constitution and a parliament to Baghdad and played midwife to the birth of Arab nationalism in Mesopotamia and throughout the Middle East.

THE SAFAVID DYNASTY (1509–1534)

Although the true origins of the Safavids are uncertain, they invaded Mesopotamia from Persia (modern Iran) in 1509. The Persians possessed an Indo-European heritage and spoke a different language than the Arabs of Mesopotamia, causing immediate tensions between the two groups. Later, they would be further divided between the Mesopotamian Sunnis and the Persian Shiites. They claimed to be descendants of Safi al-Din, an Azerbaijanian cleric. Safi al-Din was the founder the Sufi sect of Islam, which started as a branch of Shiites, although today there are Sunnis who have embraced Sufism. However, the tension between Shiite-dominated Persia and the Sunnis of Iraq still exists today.

The Sufis reject worldly goods and opulence and lead a simple life as an example to others. They believe in spirituality and self-discipline as the path to enlightenment. The word "sufi" itself means "wool" and probably originated from the intentional simplicity of the Sufis garments.

The famous whirling dervishes, called Mevlevi in Arabic, are Sufis who twirl as they chant the names of God. The popular Islamic poet Jalaluddin Rumi was a Sufi Muslim. Most Sufis were very devout Muslims, although some took their simplicity to extremes. These extremists made many Muslims distrustful and suspicious of the Sufis. No doubt others were not enticed by the Sufi doctrine eschewing worldly possessions. Sufis thrive even today, although the unfortunate prejudice against them still lingers in some Islamic countries.

For the Safavids, a large part of the enticement of Mesopotamia was control over An Najaf and Karbala, where Ali's sons were martyred and which Shiite Muslims revere as holy sites. Shah Ismail peacefully seized Baghdad in 1508. However, his armies zealously murdered Sunni Muslims and destroyed several Sunni holy sites, including the tombs of Abu Hanifa and Abdelkader al-Guiliani. The Safavids even expelled the family of al-Guiliani from Mesopotamia. Al-Guiliani was the founder of the first sect of Sufi Islam and is revered as one of the foremost Sunni saints. These draconian actions by the conquering Safavids caused the Mesopotamian Sunnis to seethe with resentment.

After declaring Shiite the official form of Islam and outlawing Sunni practices, Shah Ismail returned to Persia. His viceroy managed to keep control of Baghdad until Shah Ismail's death in 1524. By 1534, Mesopotamia would pass into Ottoman control.

INTRODUCTION TO THE OTTOMAN EMPIRE

The Ottomans are descendants of the nomadic Turkish tribes, who originated in the grasslands on the Chinese–Mongolian border. These early Turks were a nomadic people who herded goats, cattle, and sheep. Eventually, the tribes settled in Anatolia (modern-day

Turkey) and adopted Islam as their religion. The conversion to Islam greatly changed Turkish culture and way of life. Islam required worshipping one god and following a caliph rather than the tribal chief and occasionally, when the Turkish tribes united, khans. Like the Mongols, the Turks were known for their military prowess and skilled horsemanship.

Although they were generally independent and operated in autonomous tribes, by 1299 the Turkish tribes united under Osman (Othman), who ruled from 1281 to 1326. Originally, Osman was a vassal to the Seljuk Turks, but when the Seljuks were exhausted from struggling to repel the Mongols, Osman was able to take power. It is possible that the term "Ottoman" is a derivation of his name. His son, Orhan, became the first Ottoman sultan and created an empire from the remains of the Byzantine Empire. In all, 36 sultans ruled over the Ottoman Empire from 1300 to 1922. Over time, the Ottomans expanded their empire to include most of Asia Minor, the Mediterranean coast of Africa, and parts of Europe.

From 1326, the Ottomans ruled from their first capital at Bursa. In 1453, the Ottomans, led by Mehmet I, laid siege to Constantinople, the Christian capital of the Byzantine Empire. With the use of technologically advanced weapons, the Ottomans were able to use canons to breach the well-fortified walls of the city. After 54 days, the Ottomans successfully captured Constantinople, thus ending the Byzantine Empire. For the next 450 years, the Ottomans would rule their vast empire from their capital at Constantinople, now called Istanbul, meaning "city of Islam." The famous Eastern Orthodox church of Santa Sophia was converted to a mosque. Istanbul was strategically located at the point where Europe and Asia intersected and thus brought enormous wealth to the Ottoman Empire. Over time, the Ottomans created a bustling metropolis filled with mosques, madrassas, public hospitals, public baths, and marketplaces.

Mehmet I's palace was called Topkapi and was the palace of the Ottoman sultans from 1465 to 1856. Topkapi was the seat of power for the entire Ottoman Empire and was comprised of a sprawling complex of buildings and courtyards, including the Inner and Outer Palace as well as a harem for the sultan's female relatives. During the reign of Suliaman the Magnificent, Topkapi was home to more than 5,000 people. Because the gate of the grand vizier's quarters was called the Sublime Porte, foreigners often referred to the entire Ottoman Empire as the Porte. Topkapi also served as the training ground for leaders at the Palace School.

Mehmet I was a canny military leader and formed the first Ottoman navy. Through the use of the navy, Mehmet and his successors were able to gain control of the Black Sea and the eastern Mediterranean and thus create great wealth for the empire.

Though Mehmet I was a Muslim, he proclaimed tolerance for Christians and Jews, thus ensuring peace within his empire. The Ottomans allowed conquered people to retain their cultural identity and religion as long as they paid taxes and remained loyal to the sultan and to the Ottoman Empire. It is significant to note that only non-Muslims paid a personal tax, which placed an economic burden on non-Muslims, especially in times of strife or decline.

The Ottomans were devout Muslims. By the time of Sultan Selim in 1500, the Ottomans also held the caliphate and were thus leaders of the Islamic world. However, the Ottoman sultans generally claimed only secular authority and left religious matters to the learned Islamic imams. Only the Safavids of Persia challenged Ottoman supremacy and their hold on the caliphate.

Their legal system was based on the sharia, Islamic law derived from the Quran. Although the sultan was the supreme ruler and issued laws called *kanuns*, all his decisions were subject to Islamic law. On a practical level, the legal system was run by learned Islamic clerics, called muftis. Non-Muslims were permitted to follow their own religious laws and customs.

The Ottoman government was based on a military model. The sultan held the ultimate power, although he was influenced by a number of advisers, called viziers. As a group, this council of advisers made up the Divan. The principal adviser to the sultan was called the grand vizier. More than once in Ottoman history, the grand vizier acquired sufficient power to overthrow the sultan. The sultan was the only birthright position. In all other senses, Ottoman society was a meritocracy—as long as one was a Muslim, one could attain any position. Thus, complicated genealogies and old family lineages held considerably less prestige in Ottoman times than during the prior Abbasid era.

Muslims could be pressed into military service if required by the sultan. Soldiers were rewarded for their service with grants of land, and these landowners became officers. Not surprisingly, military officers were generally quite loyal to the sultan, as land equated to riches in the Ottoman world. Distinguished military officers were chosen as governors to preside over the Ottoman Empire's far-flung provinces.

Slaves were also pressed into military service. Some slaves were captured from defeated foes, but most came from a unique Ottoman practice called *devshirme,* under which non-Muslim families were required to give a male child to the sultan. These children were converted to Islam and trained in trades or crafts. Others joined the soldier corps. Occasionally, a *devshirme* even rose to the position of grand vizier to the sultan. Slave soldiers could accumulate vast wealth and power during their lifetimes. However, on their death, the wealth reverted to the crown.

Some *devshirme* children joined the elite Janissary Corps. The Janissaries were the sultan's special guard and formed an elite military service called the Praetorian Guard. They were not allowed to marry (until the 1650s) and were part of the Bektashi Islamic order. The Janissaries often wielded significant power in the far-flung Ottoman provinces. Some were even appointed governors of the provinces. Because the Janissaries possessed unique access to the sultan, they could easily overthrow an unpopular sultan or vizier. At several crucial points during the Ottoman Empire, the Janissaries revolted. Not surprisingly, this power struggle led to tension and distrust between the sultan and his guards.

One issue that plagued the rule of the Ottomans was the order of succession to the throne. In a holdover custom from the Mongol khans, any son of the sultan could succeed his father to the throne. Therefore, when the sultan died, fierce power struggles would break out among the sultan's sons, and fratricide was common. Occasionally, sons tired of awaiting their father's death and committed patricide, as in the case of Selim I, who murdered his father, Beyazit II, in 1512. Succession would be in question for months or even years at a time, and multiple "courts" were common. Although eventually a primogeniture system was established, the succession conundrum and resulting dissension ultimately weakened the Ottoman Empire.

THE OTTOMANS IN MESOPOTAMIA (1534–1915)

A Kurdish leader, Dhul-Figar, then wrested control of Baghdad and eventually the rest of Mesopotamia from the Persians. To prevent Safavid vengeance, Dhul-Figar brokered an agreement in which he proclaimed his liege to the Ottoman ruler, Sultan Sulaiman the Magnificent. But this agreement was not enough to prevent the Persians from capturing Baghdad again in 1530 and slaying

Dhul-Figar. In Mesopotamia, the Ottoman sultan wanted revenge for the murder of his vassal, Dhul-Figar, and for the massacre of the Sunni populace. Much of the tension between Sunnis and Shiites results from the division between the Shiite Safavids and the Ottoman Sunnis. Sultan Sulaiman (Sulayman) the Magnificent took Baghdad without bloodshed in 1534 after the Safavid ruler fled the city. By 1538, Sulaiman took the southern Mesopotamian cities, including the profitable Persian Gulf port of Basra. All of Mesopotamia was now under Ottoman dominion. From this point forward, Mesopotamia was an Ottoman province. In practical terms, the Ottomans were not able to control the rural areas, which were controlled by various tribal leaders.

The great-grandson of Mehmet II, Sulaiman (1520–1566), ruled over the belle epoque of the Ottoman Empire. Sulaiman rebuilt the tombs of Abu-Hanifa and al-Guiliani before departing Baghdad. As the Ottomans favored indirect rule over their conquered territories, Sulaiman installed a system of Ottoman governors. Over time, the Sunnis from the Sunni triangle around Baghdad came to dominate the political affairs of Mesopotamia. Sulaiman was famous for his Ottoman law codes. By combining Islamic religious laws with every-day legal issues, he created a unified legal code that he imposed throughout the empire.

He also brought great prosperity to the Ottoman Empire via his brilliant military conquests and control over lucrative trade routes and industries, especially the coffee trade and the silk trade. The Ottomans sat at the crossroads between the East and West, and therefore goods passing between China and Europe traveled through Ottoman-controlled territory. The Ottomans built rest stops for travelers called caravansaries and policed the trade routes to discourage thieves, pirates, and bandits. Every transaction made along these sales routes were taxed and thus brought enormous wealth to the Ottoman coffers. Sulaiman encouraged trade with Europe and thus brought diversity and technological advances to the Ottomans.

Arts, architecture, and culture blossomed under Sulaiman's rule. Sulaiman himself was the author of more than 3,000 poems. Calligraphy and detailed miniature paintings were hallmarks of the Ottoman Empire. The enormous Suleymaniye Mosque, designed by famed *devshirme* architect Mimar Sinan to specifically outshine the vast Santa Sophia church, still overlooks the Bosporus River and the Golden Horn harbor in Istanbul today. Sinan's architecture is noted for his sublimely decorated minarets, which still rise over Istanbul. In Sulaiman's time, the Suleymaniye Mosque was an impressive complex of buildings, including madrassas, libraries, a hospital, and a caravansary. Many artisans' guilds sprang up throughout the empire, and the government set strict price controls for the artisans' wares. The craftsmen displayed their wares in the Grand Market in Istanbul, a sprawling wonderland of exotic crafts, spices, and luxury goods.

After Sulaiman's death in battle in 1566, the Ottoman Empire began a gradual decline. Overtaxation and reliance on slaves as soldiers, as well as the extravagant lifestyle of the sultan and his court, created unrest and resentment among the Ottoman populace.

In 1622, insurgents, led by Janissary leader Bekr Agha and aligned with the Persian Safavid Shah Abbas, staged a coup and murdered the Ottoman governor in Baghdad. Bekr Agha then double-crossed Shah Abbas and struck a bargain with the ruling sultan that allowed Bekr Agha to be governor of Baghdad. This duplicity enraged Shah Abbas, and the Safavids laid siege to Baghdad. Within three months, Baghdad again fell into Persian hands. Once again, Sunnis were murdered, and the tombs of Abu-Hanifa and al-Guiliani were destroyed. The Ottomans retained control of the northern Mesopotamian city of Mosul, which they used as a base to attack the Safavids.

Despite the best efforts of the Ottomans, the Safavids retained control of Baghdad until 1638, when Sultan Murad IV led 10,000 troops to recapture Baghdad. The Ottomans and the Safavids fought at Samara, and Sultan Murad IV chased the retreating Safavids all the way to Baghdad. The Ottomans blockaded the city and took the city after a 40-day siege. From this point forward, Mesopotamia would remain an Ottoman province until World War I. In 1639, the Safavids and the Ottomans agreed to a peace treaty that established the boundary between Mesopotamia and Persia that exists to this day.

During Ottoman rule, Mesopotamia was called the "Principality of Baghdad," which encompassed all of modern Mesopotamia and Kuwait. The three main Ottoman provinces, called *vilayets*, were the northern area of Mosul, the middle Mesopotamian region of Baghdad, and the southern area known as Basra. A series of governors, called *pashas*, governed Baghdad and essentially operated autonomously and independently from Istanbul. The pasha of Baghdad struggled to control the independent countryside tribes who wreaked havoc with the caravans passing along Mesopotamia's extensive trade routes.

In 1683, the Turks again tried to capture Vienna, Austria, and again were unsuccessful. From this point forward, the Ottoman Empire began a long, slow slide into decay and decline. The empire even earned the sobriquet the "sick man of Europe" as European nations and the birth of nationalism in Arab countries began to encroach on Ottoman territory. In the European mind, the Turks became associated with treachery and cruelty.

In the 1700s, the Ottoman Empire began interacting with the West and attempting to imitate various Western institutions, social movements, and technological advances. Sultan Ahmet III (1703–1730) sent his grand vizier to discover technological advances in France, then on the cusp of the Industrial Revolution. He introduced the printing press to the Ottomans, ushering in an age of learning and literacy that transformed the Ottoman Empire. The vizier also brought back the tulip, and Ahmet was captivated by it. He built enormous palaces and flower gardens devoted to the tulip and instituted a yearly festival during the spring blooming season. Ahmet was dubbed the "Tulip King" and his reign the "Tulip period." Unfortunately, the Janissaries became frustrated with Ahmet's apparent lack of interest in military conquest and, during a 1730 riot, deposed and imprisoned him.

The late 1700s and 1800s were a time of great reform throughout the Ottoman Empire as the sultans struggled to institute the government reforms so popular in Europe and take steps toward democracy. Collectively, these reforms were known as the Tanzimat, meaning "reorganization." Traditional Muslims resisted the reforms, and the reformed-minded populace considered them insufficient, leaving the ruling Ottomans in an untenable position.

After Napoleon's invasion of Egypt in 1798, the ruling sultan, Selim III, tried to introduce reforms, especially against corruption in the military ranks. In 1807, the Janissaries assassinated him. His successor, Mahmud II, instituted a cabinet and encouraged education in the sciences, which some considered a threat to the traditional Islamic lifestyle. He also abolished the traditional turban and instead required that Muslim men wear a fez, which became a symbol of reform.

As stated previously, the Janissaries wielded enormous power throughout the Ottoman Empire. Perhaps fearing the fate of his predecessor, Sultan Mahmud II ordered the massacre of the Janissaries in 1826. Another class of slave-warriors, the Mamluks from Buywaid times, rose to power beginning in the 1750s. They worked from within the Ottoman government and were able to wrest control from the tribal sheiks and consolidate governance of the *vilayets* of Basra and Baghdad. In 1831, the Ottomans reclaimed their power from the Mamluks, but it was not until the 1860s that the Ottomans truly gained control over all of Mesopotamia again.

The 1800s were a time of shrinking power and influence for the Ottoman Empire as its conquered lands struggled for independence. Russia was a significant threat to Ottoman rule, especially in the Balkans. The Russians wanted access to the Black Sea as part of lucrative economic trade routes. Although the Ottomans were able to hold the region during and after the Crimean War, they lost control of the Black Sea region by 1878. These losses created economic hardship throughout the empire and caused the Ottomans to levy greater taxes and tributes throughout their remaining lands. This economic strife was a direct cause of the decline of the Ottoman Empire.

In 1831, the bubonic plague struck Baghdad and decimated the population. Additionally, religious tensions between the Russian Eastern Orthodox Church and the Islamic power of the Ottomans caused the Balkans region to reach the boiling point. During the 1800s, the Ottomans lost control of several Balkan states, including Greece, Serbia, and Romania. Quieting these internal rebellions and the loss of territory throughout the 1800s weakened the once-mighty empire.

From 1869 to 1872, governor Midhat Pasha introduced many reforms to Mesopotamia, including a revised legal system, an educational system, and easily available health care. He founded Mesopotamia's first newspaper. Many of these reforms were in response to the Industrial Revolution in Europe and the United States. By mass-producing less expensive goods, the Europeans overtook native manufacturers, leading to economic hardship throughout the shrinking Ottoman Empire and creating significant dependence on imported goods.

REVOLUTION OF THE YOUNG TURKS

In 1895, the Committee of Union and Progress (CUP) was formed by a group of young government officials anxious to change the Ottoman government from within. They were increasingly beginning to develop an Arabic self-identity in contrast to the Turkish Ottomans and the Shiite Persians. The increasing influence of Great Britain, which coveted a more efficient connection to its precious Indian colony as well as the vast oil reserves beneath the Mesopotamian sands, and Germany, which wanted to create a transcontinental railway between Baghdad and Berlin, also concerned the new Arab nationalists.

The CUP wished to make the empire democratic with a written constitution and an elected assembly. The CUP's leaders, dubbed the Young Turks, were well-educated, wealthy merchants, scholars, and religious leaders. They resented the foreign administration of their homeland and sought independence from foreign rule.

On July 24, 1908, the Young Turks were successful in their quest to obtain a constitution and parliament for Mesopotamia. However, their success was short lived. With the advent of World War I, the Young Turks' hope for a democratic future was dashed.

When World War I began, the Allies—Great Britain, France, and Russia—banded together against the Central Powers—Austria and Germany. The Ottomans joined the Central Powers, hoping to defeat their longtime nemesis, Russia.

By 1916, the British held Mesopotamia, thus ending more than 400 years of Ottoman control. When the Treaty of Sevres was agreed to in 1920 between the victorious Allies and the Ottoman sultan, the outline of present-day Iraq emerged.

In 1922, Mustafa Kemal won Turkish independence from Greek occupiers. He eradicated the sultanate and disbanded the Ottoman Empire. When the Republic of Turkey was formed in 1923, the Ottoman Empire officially came to an end. However, the influence of this massive, sprawling empire endures as a bridge between East and West. Turkoman descendants of the Ottomans still call Iraq home.

6

The British Occupation

Although Great Britain desired control of Iraqi oil reserves and trade shipping routes for more than a century, the opportunity did not arise until the start of World War I. Iraq was the scene of fierce fighting between the British and the Germans during World War I. In 1920, the British were given the mandate of all Iraq. Mesopotamia became known as Iraq from this point forward. After the insurrection of 1920, the British governed Iraq by proxy and set Faisal I as king of Iraq in 1921.

British imperialism in Iraq caused issues that still affect Iraq today. Significantly, the British granted Sunni Muslims control over Iraq, infuriating the Shiite majority and inflaming tensions that still exist. The heavy-handed British also fostered Iraqi resentment to non-Iraqi rulers and occupying regimes and created a seething cauldron of anti-Western animus.

THE BRITISH IN IRAQ

As industrialization progressed, the world developed an apparently unquenchable thirst for oil. As early as the 1870s, vast oil deposits were discovered under the sands of Iraq. However, it was not until the turn of the twentieth century that the true value and importance of the subterranean black gold was understood. More and more industries—such as those of the automobile and airplane—required great quantities of oil. Winston Churchill, the Lord of the Admiralty of the British Royal Navy, decreed that the British navy would begin powering its ships using oil. From this point forward, Great Britain, which possessed no oil reserves of its own, began coveting Iraqi oil and would begin to challenge Ottoman dominion over Iraq.

The discovery of oil was not the only reason that Great Britain was interested in annexing Iraq. At first, the British were interested in protecting their prime colony, India. The East India Company exchanged goods with India via the Red Sea and with Asia through Afghanistan. However, the trade routes to India transversing Iraq are significantly shorter and therefore were very desirable to the British Empire. Additionally, the British wanted control of the airspace to India and also to have secure refueling outposts in the Middle East. Iraq was the perfect location to help Great Britain hold India.

The British did not arrive in Iraq at the start of World War I in 1914. They manned a trade outpost in Basra by the seventeenth century, and soon the "resident" consulate became a very powerful and influential adviser to the Ottoman pasha. British companies and industry were welcomed in Iraq, and steam navigation became a significant economic boon to the region.

The Germans were interested in Iraqi oil as early as 1871 but declared it virtually impossible to harvest. However, the Germans were not without influence in Baghdad. By 1894, Kaiser Wilhelm II of Germany appointed a consul to Baghdad and to Mosul. Much to the dismay of the British, who sought to protect their exclusive trade routes in Iraq, Wilhelm II struck an agreement with Sultan Abdul Hamid to construct a railway to connect the Turkish city of Konya to Baghdad. Eventually, the Ottomans agreed to extend the railway to the Iraqi port city of Basra. The Germans wanted to extend the railroad into Kuwait and from Konya to Berlin. In addition to the rights to build the railway, Wilhelm II was able to obtain the right to exploratory drilling along the planned railway route and also began planning agricultural colonies. These colonies would have provided much-needed food to the population of Iraq and helped to cure the oversalinization and overfarming of the soil that still plague Iraq today.

Needless to say, the British were less than delighted with the German intrusion into Iraq. The British, in turn, obtained the majority rights to a Turkish oil refinery on the Shatt al-Arab. By 1901, the British reached an agreement with the Ottomans to export oil from Ottoman territories, including Iraq, in exchange for British military protection. In 1912, the British formed two oil companies to pump oil in Ottoman-controlled regions. The Turkish Petroleum Company harvested oil in the province of Iraq, especially in the area around Mosul.

The British continued their efforts to train the Iraqi army, install a telegraph system, and conduct topographical surveys. During this period and then following World War I, British archaeologists descended on Iraq and began the archaeological digs that give us the history of ancient Mesopotamia. By infiltrating nearly every level of Iraqi society, the British were able to minimize German influence and to conduct intelligence gathering among Iraqi society. This knowledge would prove invaluable in the coming World War I.

Iraq during World War I

Once Great Britain found Germany and the Ottomans as their foes in World War I, they moved quickly to secure Iraq. After all, their Turkish Petroleum Company was now in enemy territory. On November 6, 1914, the British military arrived in Iraq at Faw. They took Basra on November 22 and advanced toward Baghdad. However, the Germans had allied with the rural tribes, and the Ottomans launched a fierce counterattack against the British. The British were forced to retreat from Ctesiphon and take refuge at al-Kut, a small town on the Tigris River.

Thomas Edward Lawrence, known as "Lawrence of Arabia," was a British Military Intelligence Service officer who organized the Iraqi tribes into fighting forces to assist the British during World War I. Lawrence was also great friends with Prince Faisal, who would be crowned king of Iraq in 1921. When the British refused to grant their Arab allies their promised independence, Lawrence resigned his commission in protest. However, despite his best efforts during the war, he was unable to calm the Iraqi tribes enraged by the British advance toward Baghdad. Having chafed so long under the yoke of the Ottomans, the Iraqis were exasperated by what they perceived as yet another foreign occupation.

Another British figure with enormous influence in the Middle East was Gertrude Bell. She was fluent in Arabic and had excavated several major archaeological sites in Mesopotamia before the war. During World War I, she was the only female intelligence officer employed by the British in their Cairo-based Arab Bureau, where she worked to gain intelligence about the Arab opposition to Turkey. She was nicknamed "Daughter of the Desert" by the Arabs whom she tried to unite against the Ottomans. After the war, she served as "Oriental Secretary" to the British government in Iraq. Later, she became known as the "Uncrowned Queen of Iraq" because of her relationship with King Faisal I as a personal and political adviser. She was also the only woman to attend Winston Churchill's Conference of Cairo in 1921. She is credited with starting the Baghdad Museum and led the collection of antiquities and archaeological finds that are still on display there.

After a five-month siege of the British at al-Kut, the Turks and the British met at Ctesiphon. The Turks won a decisive victory, and the British began to retreat toward their supply base at Basra. General Townsend rallied his men to a last stand against the Turks at al-Kut. By April 1916, more than 13,000 British and Indian soldiers were taken prisoner, including General Townsend. Although Townsend was able to serve out his captivity in Istanbul, some 4,000 of his troops would die in captivity before the end of the war.

In June 1916, by promising to create a great Arab kingdom, the British were able to persuade some Arabs under the control of Sharif Hussein of Mecca to join the Allies. Stung by their crushing defeat the previous year, the British sent troops, under the command of General Stanley Maude, up the Tigris River to take Baghdad by surprise and stealth on March 11, 1917. On March 19, Maude issued a proclamation that he and the British were committed to the self-governance of the Iraqi people after the end of the war. Maude's proclamation requested Arab assistance with overthrowing the Ottomans and with Arabic support. After making his promises, Maude was able to secure the Iraqi countryside.

Maude's proclamation and the British assurances to Sharif Hussein were in direct contrast to the secret French/British pact: the 1916 Sykes-Picot Agreement. In this agreement, between Sir Mark Sykes of Great Britain and François Georges-Picot of France, the British and French, with the concurrence of Russia, agreed to divide up the Ottoman territories into "zones of influence" at the conclusion of hostilities. The Turkish areas affected included Syria, Iraq, Lebanon, and Palestine. According to the map that accompanied the Sykes-Picot Agreement, France would control Syria, Lebanon, and the province of Mosul, while Great Britain would gain dominion over the provinces of Basra and Baghdad. Great Britain also received control of Palestinian ports.

The armistice with Turkey was signed on November 3, 1918, and some five days later Maude and his troops took oil-rich Mosul. In the Sykes-Picot Agreement, Mosul was supposed to belong to the French, but the British claimed it was necessary to secure the oil fields in the region. The British began negotiations with the French president, Georges Clemenceau, for control of Mosul (and thus much of Iraqi oil production). Initially, it was agreed that the British could hold the city as long as the French were permitted to conduct oil exploration in Mosul.

The British Mandate in Iraq

The Treaty of Versailles ended World War I, and the future of the Middle East was settled at the Conference of San Remo in April 1920. Under the agreement brokered at San Remo, the League of Nations was to administer and govern the territories of the defeated Ottomans and Germans. The territories, now called mandates, were to be controlled by the European allies until the mandates were able to govern themselves. By the close of the San Remo Conference, the British held the power of mandate over all of Iraq.

As part of the agreement at San Remo, new national and regional borders were drawn for each mandate. These essentially amounted to straight lines drawn on the Middle East map, with little consideration or interest in traditional boundaries or local realities. The new borders crisscrossed the desert and divided local tribes and clans as well as inadvertently placing rival tribes under the same mandate.

These arbitrarily drawn borders caused strife throughout the Middle East but were particularly disastrous for Iraq. In the south, the new country of Kuwait was created, named for a prominent trading city there. The city of Kuwait had long been a trading partner for the Iraqi port city of Basra. With the creation of Kuwait, the Iraqi coastline shrunk, making exports much more difficult. Additionally, the British created a diamond-shaped neutral zone between Iraq and Saudi Arabia that became contentious when the question of who controlled the oil reserves in the neutral zone arose. Perhaps most significantly, the British had no empathy or understanding of the cultural impact of combining the Shiite and Sunni segments of the country. Initially, Mosul was not considered part of the British Mandate but was added in 1925 when the new country of Turkey tried to claim the oil-rich area. Under the terms of the mandate, Iraq was granted "Class A" status, meaning that the country was to achieve independence quickly.

The Iraqis were dismayed that the Allies, especially the British, did not assist their Arab allies in the immediate creation of independent Arab nations, something that they believed was promised to them during the war. After the Treaty of Versailles, most Arab leaders believed that the intent was to create immediate nations out of the conquered Ottoman territories. To add insult to injury, the British made no efforts to align themselves with the local Arab leaders but instead partnered with the Ottoman rulers and elite who remained in Iraq.

The British intended to rule by proxy and set up a temporary government until their mandate was complete. The British modeled their oversight and the Iraqi government on their methods in British-controlled India. Iraq was divided into districts that were nominally run by an Iraqi governor. In reality, the British kept control. Each Iraqi officer was given a British counterpart who held the actual authority. The British abolished the Ottoman government and rules and replaced it with British models. They instituted a new civil and criminal code based on common law rather than the Ottoman Islamic-based codes (this decision was later reversed). The currency was the Indian rupee, and the Iraqi military was replaced with a new army and police force made up mostly of Indians. The British inadvertently strengthened tribal bonds by relying on tribal sheiks to control the restless rural Arabs.

However, the British were soon to discover that the Kurdish-controlled northern provinces were not easily governed. During World War I, the British promised the Kurds that they would help set up a Kurdish nation in return for the Kurds' assistance against the Ottomans. The British had also promised the same land to their Arab allies. The end result was that the Kurds were separated into three countries (Iran, Iraq, and Turkey) and possessed no independent state of their own. When Mosul was incorporated into the Iraqi state in 1925, the Kurds living in that area were incorporated into Iraq. To further complicate matters, the British had also promised independence to the Assyrians of northwestern Iraq. The British gave the Assyrians sanctuary inside the traditional Kurdish territories, causing further tension with the Kurds. The broken British promise to the Kurds has reverberated throughout modern Iraq's history and is still a contentious issue today.

By May 1919, the Kurdish sheik Mahmud took Sulaimaniya and proclaimed himself "King of Kurdistan." To quell this uprising, the British used poison gas and bombardments. The savage response of the British fanned the flames of the Iraqi independence movement and set the stage for the Rebellion of 1920.

The Rebellion of 1920

In the late spring and early summer of 1920, the British Mandate of Iraq and the agreements struck in the San Remo conference became clear to the Iraqis. Anti-British sentiment had been simmering, and Iraqis desired freedom for British rule and oversight. The Rebellion of 1920 marked the first time that Sunnis and Shiites banded together and cooperated to attempt to free their country from a foreign overlord.

In June 1920, the British arrested a tribal sheik in a small town near the middle of the Euphrates River for failing to pay agricultural debts. Enraged, the sheik's tribe and other Arab sympathizers stormed the prison and freed him. By July, tribal unrest was so prevalent that the British barricaded themselves in Baghdad and awaited reinforcements. The Rebellion of 1920 was led by secret societies comprised of Iraqi elites and began in Mosul. The siege, which lasted approximately three months, resulted in significant casualties for the British (estimates are as high as 2,200 dead) and massive casualties for the Iraqis. The uprisings were confined mostly to the countryside tribes and failed to take root in the cities. The British believed that the uprisings were a complex plot by the Germans, Turks, and Russian Bolsheviks. However, the true significance of the 1920 uprising was that the Iraqis were working together across tribal, cultural, traditional, and religious boundaries to oust the occupying British forces.

After the Rebellion of 1920, the British realized that proxy governance would not work in Iraq for long and that the increasingly expensive mandate needed to end. They also realized that the Indian model of imperial governance did not transfer well to Iraq. In order to complete their mandate, Iraq needed to gain independence as quickly as possible. The British, however, had no intention of leaving Iraq entirely or passing control of Iraq's rich oil fields to an independent government. But, from the end of the July insurrection, the British knew that their influence would have to be behind the scenes.

Sir Percy Cox was appointed as the first high commissioner of Iraq and was instructed to create an Arab state and Arab government, complete with a constitution, a council of state, and an Arab president. Cox's assistant, Colonel Arnold Talbot Wilson, soon took over. Wilson's background was as an imperial administrator in India, and he soon installed a number of Indians to oversee the Iraqi government rather than entrusting administrative duties to the Iraqis. Not surprisingly, the Iraqis were considerably displeased and alienated by Wilson's actions.

The Conference of Cairo

In March 1921, T. E. Lawrence, Sir Percy Cox, Gertrude Bell, and Winston Churchill gathered along with other British political luminaries and Middle East scholars at the Semiramis hotel in Cairo. The purpose of the Conference of Cairo was to decide on the political and militaristic future of the Middle East and also to minimize the growing cost of the British occupation of Iraq. Newly appointed Colonial Secretary Churchill chaired the gathering. The Conference of Cairo established the foundation of Iraqi government by creating the Iraqi monarchy, a democratic-based constitution, and a treaty granting the legal basis for Great Britain's continued dominion over Iraq.

In order to keep their controlling influence, the British needed to install an Arab leader in Iraq who was pro-British. What they eventually did was establish pro-British monarchies throughout the Middle East—in Jordan, Iraq, and Syria. "Churchill's scheme was, in effect, to establish a series of pro-British client monarchies, all of whose rulers would owe Britain a debt of considerable gratitude simply for the fact that they were in power at all."[1]

For their Iraqi leader, they looked no further than the son of the Hashemite Hussein ibn Ali, the sharif of Mecca. The Ottoman sultan appointed the holder of the sharif of Mecca, and the sharif held considerable influence in the Islamic community, especially among Sunni Muslims. The Hashemite family enjoyed considerable power and influence in the Arab world. His son, Faisal, was a British-educated man who understood the culture of the Western world. He was a close ally of Lawrence of Arabia and Gertrude Bell and had been king of Syria for a year before the French Mandate took effect there. The Hashemites were of the Quraishi tribe and therefore claimed a lineage all the way back to the Prophet Muhammad. The British assumed, incorrectly, that the Hashemite family name and ancestry would legitimize the rule of Faisal in Iraq. While the Sunni population did recognize Faisal's religious authority (in the Sunni worldview, as a descendant of Muhammad and the sharif of Mecca, Faisal would have been eligible to hold the caliphate), the Shiites did not recognize the authority of Hussein ibn Ali and, in fact, sought a more theocratic form of government. More important, the Hashemites were not Iraqi and were therefore viewed by the Iraqi populace as invaders.

Winston Churchill, as chairman of the Conference of Cairo, named Faisal to be the future king of Iraq at the conference. The British were careful to keep their choice of Faisal secret so as to prevent Faisal's being seen as a tool of the British. On June 21, 1921, Faisal arrived in Baghdad. A voting referendum was organized, with one question on the ballot, and Faisal received 96 percent of the vote, which, to the British at least, allowed him legitimacy to take the throne. On August 27, 1921, Faisal I was crowned king of Iraq.

With Faisal came the Arab nationalists—well-educated Arab lawyers, army officers, and civil servants—who served beside him in World War I and in his Syrian government. These men were completely loyal to Faisal and brought Sunni leadership throughout the Iraqi government.

The British thought that this would allow for better foreign relationships with the Sunni-dominated countries surrounding Iraq and allow for easier oil exportation. However, they did not consider that the Shiites were (and remain) the majority population in Iraq. The Sunnis emphasized a secular, Arab nationalist worldview and, as such, were anathema to the Iraqi Shiites. Additionally, their promotion of a pan-Arab identity undercut the development of an Iraqi national identity, a problem that still plagues Iraqi society today.

Additionally, the British decided to assist in the formation of an Iraqi army, drawn from native Iraqis, rather than the hired Indian force of recent years. The rank-and-file military men were drawn from the poorer Shiite tribes, and well-educated Sunnis were installed as officers, further perpetuating the Islamic divide.

As part of the discussion of the Conference of Cairo, the British considered establishing a Kurdish state as a buffer state between Turkey and Iraq. However, the conference saw Iraqi national unity as a more important factor, and thus the Kurds were denied their promised homeland. Another proposal was entertained to split Iraq into two separate kingdoms along the provinces of Baghdad and Basra. Instead, the northern Kurds, the Baghdad-based Sunni Muslims, and the southern-based Shiites were joined into one country.

One of Faisal's first actions was to enter into treaty negotiations with the British. The treaty, conceived at the Conference of Cairo and ratified by the Iraqi Council of Ministers in October 1922, was to legitimize the British influence in Iraq. Set to last for 20 years, the treaty guaranteed that the Iraqi government would consult with the British on foreign affairs, on fiscal policy (including oil exportation), and on all matters affecting British interests. The terms of the treaty also required that the Iraqis allow British "advisers" to be installed through the Iraqi government, thus setting up an effective British intelligence network throughout the Iraqi state. The British promised considerable financial and military aid to Iraq and also sponsorship to the League of Nations. In essence, the treaty was the formal mechanism through which the British executed their post–World War I mandate.

The Iraqi constitution was another means for the British to assert their influence. Ratified in 1924, the Iraqi constitution delineated the powers of the king and parliament. Although the powers were somewhat balanced, the British-supported king was able to dominate the Iraqi nationalist–controlled parliament through his right to confirm all parliamentary laws and to call for elections. The constitution stood as the law of the land until the Revolution of 1958.

NOTE

1. Christopher Catherwood, *Churchill's Folly: How Winston Churchill Created Modern Iraq* (New York: Carroll & Graf, 2004), p. 141.

7

The Kingdom of Iraq and
the Revolution of 1958

As discussed in chapter 6, the 1921 Conference of Cairo created the British-backed Kingdom of Iraq. In 1932, Iraq was admitted to the League of Nations, thus ending the British Mandate following World War I. However, Great Britain still enjoyed great influence in Iraq's affairs until the Revolution of 1958. In July 1958, the Iraqi monarchy was overthrown, and British influence ended.

THE KINGDOM OF IRAQ

As discussed in the previous chapter, Faisal I ascended to the Iraqi throne in 1921. He was backed and assisted by the British, who, after World War I, held a mandate over Iraq. Faisal presided over a difficult and turbulent period in Iraqi history and faced the nearly impossible task of reconciling British requirements and local demands. The British would not allow him to be much more than London's puppet, while the increasingly important Arab nationalists in Iraq resented and resisted British influence. The 1921

Conference of Cairo created the monarchy that Faisal I headed but also incorporated the Kurds, the Sunnis, and the Shiites into one country, with little to no consideration for ancient tribal factions or traditional boundaries. Initially, Mosul was not part of the British Mandate over Iraq but rather was under joint British and French control. However, after oil was discovered in Mosul and when the northern Turks menaced the territory, the British incorporated Mosul into Iraq in 1925. Modern Iraq still incorporates Mosul.

In 1922, Faisal mysteriously fell ill, and Sir Percy Cox, the former British high commissioner, took over the handling of affairs of the Iraqi state for a time. Cox took steps to minimize the rising tide of nationalist sentiment, such as deporting nationalist leaders and abolishing newspapers.

During the mandate, the British struggled to cope with the northern Kurds. To win the support of the Kurds during World War I, the British promised the Kurds that they would gain Mosul *vilayet* as part of an independent Kurdish state. Unfortunately, the British had also promised their Arab allies the same land as part of an independent Arab state. When these contradictory promises came to light, the Iraqis' trust in the British—never very strong—was nearly destroyed. Ultimately, the British gave the land to the Arabs, leaving the Kurds without a homeland to call their own.

Today, the Kurds still do not possess a homeland and are spread among Turkey, Iraq, and Iran. However, this dream of a homeland, which the Kurds themselves term "Kurdistan," continues to have profound effect on the politics and culture of the Middle East. The forcible incorporation of the Kurds into Iraq reverberates though modern Iraqi history and remains a contentious issue today.

In response to what the Kurds perceived as British treachery, Sheik Mahmud again attempted to take Sulaimaniya, and the British used Chaldean mercenaries to defeat him. Mahmud would continue to plague the British until the late 1920s, when he took refuge in the mountains of Persia. Mahmud's revolt did have a significant lasting impact on the country because, as a result of Mahmud's revolt, the British determined that a national Iraqi standing army was necessary to protect the new Iraqi state. This army was formed and trained by the British. The soldiers were mostly Shiites, but most officers were Sunni Muslims, which led to Shiite oppression over time.

The Arab nationalists were further provoked when the terms of the Anglo–Iraqi treaty that was developed from the Conference of Cairo came to light. The treaty was signed on October 10, 1922, under threat of return to British occupation. One element of the treaty that particularly angered the Arab nationalists was that Great Britain was to act on Iraq's behalf and represent Iraq on all foreign affairs throughout the world.

The Iraqi National Assembly that was stipulated in the Anglo–Iraqi treaty convened in 1925. Although the minority Sunnis were able to dominate the monarchy and the military, the majority Shiites held power in the legislature. However, the National Assembly was never particularly effective at exercising its power, and its legislation was only rarely enforced.

With the worldwide rise of the automobile and airplane industries, oil was increasingly important. In 1927, an enormous oil field was discovered near Kirkuk, a small village roughly equidistant from Baghdad and Mosul. Partially in response to this bounty, the Iraq Petroleum Company was created in 1928, and France held nearly 24 percent control of the corporation.

Iraqi Independence

In October 1932, Iraq was admitted to the League of Nations under the sponsorship of the British. While this officially ended the British Mandate, British influence did not end. Just less than a year later, on September 1, 1933, King Faisal died in a Swiss hospital. The cause of his death is unknown.

His successor was his eldest son, Ghazi I. Although Ghazi was educated in Great Britain, he despised the British and greatly resented British influence in Iraq. Ghazi was a strident Arab nationalist and an advocate of pan-Arabism. Briefly, pan-Arabism is a movement that supports freedom for all Arab people with the ultimate goal of a united Arab homeland. In furtherance of his pan-Arab goals, Ghazi worked to build an alliance among the Arab countries created out of Ottoman territories after World War I. For example, he brokered a treaty with his relatives, the ruling family of Saudi Arabia.

For their part, the British were not overly fond of Ghazi, either. In rejecting the British, Ghazi partnered with the Germans. Ghazi felt that Kuwait should be absorbed into the Iraqi kingdom and worked toward that goal. Although Ghazi was anti-British and thus aligned with the popular sentiment of the Iraqi people, he made no attempt to integrate Iraqis into his government and, like his father, was never truly accepted as a legitimate ruler by the Iraqis themselves. From the pan-Arab perspective, the British essentially created an artificial state and then further compounded this error by imposing a government dominated by the British and the Saudis, who would forever be resented outsiders by the Iraqis.

During this period, the Iraqi army, created by the British to defend against the Kurds, became a very powerful force in the Kingdom of Iraq. Although the army was initially loyal to the monarchy and assisted with quelling several Kurdish and Assyrian uprisings, many soldiers were from the disenfranchised Iraqi Shiites and sympathized with the Arab nationalist cause. They also viewed the Hashemite dynasty as illegitimate foreign rulers.

In 1936, in a coup, Kurdish General Bakr Sidqi became head of the army. Sidqi and his cronies assassinated the defense minister and attained power by assembling a coalition government of Kurds, Shiites, and Sunnis. Ghazi I made no effort to quash the uprising and allowed a temporary government to be appointed. Once this new government was created, the coalition cracked from within because of ideological differences. The Kurds and Shiites were focused on internal reforms, while their brethren Sunni wanted to militarily expand Iraq through conquest. Ghazi's pan-Arab efforts were virtually ignored. Although the new government was supposedly more representative of the Iraqi people, they angered the Arab nationalists by catering to the Turks and to Iran. In August 1937, Bakr Sidqi was assassinated.

Ghazi I dissolved the parliament in December 1938. By 1939, the new government began to make plans to retake Kuwait. During Ottoman times, Kuwait was considered part of Basra *vilayet,* and the new Iraqi government still considered it part of Iraq. After the outbreak of World War II, the coalition government's plans for Kuwait were abandoned but not forgotten by the Iraqis.

In April 1939, Ghazi I perished in a mysterious car accident. His eldest son, Faisal, was only four years old when he assumed the throne. Parliament reconvened to swear in Emir Abd al Ilah, a Saudi first cousin to Faisal II, as the regent. Later, the regent would support the Arab nationalists against the British. However, Bakr al Sidqi's successor, Premier Nuri as-Said, held the true power in Iraq. As-Said was also in control of the military as an army general. Five months later, on September 3, 1939, Great Britain declared war on Germany, and World War II began.

WORLD WAR II

By March 1940, Iraqis elected a new government with strong Arab nationalist sentiments. Their new premier was Rashid Ali al-Gailani. Al-Gailani wanted the British out of Iraq and to create the first independent Arab nation. As part of al-Gailani's anti-British efforts, the Anglo–Iraqi treaty was ignored. When the British sought to enforce the treaty, al-Gailani led a revolt in April 1941.

The grand mufti of Jerusalem and a group of four army officers, called the colonels of the "Golden Square," supported al-Gailani's revolt. The army officers gained control of the government, forcing Regent Emir Abdullah to flee the country. Al-Gailani and his rebels believed they would enjoy the support of Germany. However, Hitler was preoccupied with fighting Russia, and their promised support never materialized. In their defiance, al-Gailani and his men sought to limit British influence, especially British military influence, in Iraq.

Facing a difficult fight with the Germans, the British were dismayed by al-Gailani's rebellion and feared limits on their access to oil and to their premier colony, India. By using troops stationed in India and Iran, the British arrived in Basra on May 2, 1941. After about four weeks of fierce fighting, the British were able to quell the uprising and recapture Baghdad by the end of May 1941. Although al-Gailani escaped, the Golden Square colonels were executed. Al-Gailani would later play a major role in the Revolution of 1958.

After al-Gailani's rebellion was quieted, the British again backed the Hashemite monarch, Faisal II. Faisal was only six years old at this point. However, the British remained blind to the political and cultural issues that plagued the Hashemite reign. Because the Hashemites were Saudi Arabian, the Iraqis did not—and never would—view them as legitimate rulers in Iraqi. From the British perspective, they needed a monarchy that would remain pro-British and allow for continued access to precious oil and India, especially as they were now firmly entrenched in World War II. Because Great Britain was allied with Russia during World War II, Iraq also was a strategic access point during the war.

Once again, the British issued conflicting promises throughout World War II. They were able to persuade Iraq to support the alliance by dangling the carrot of increasing independence after the war. In addition, the British made contradictory promises to the Palestinians and the Jews who lived in the area of the Palestinian

Mandate after World War I. Eventually, these promises would lead to the creation of Israel, a development that Iraqis were and are firmly against.

Nuri as-Said retained power after al-Gailani's revolt and agreed to ally with the British during World War II. On January 17, 1943, Iraq formally declared war on Germany and the Axis states. During the war, as-Said and the National Assembly still vied for power with the British. The young king and his regent were virtually ignored. The British were quick to quash any attempt at self-governance during and immediately following the war. After the war, the regent and as-Said were in frequent opposition to each other. This apparent inability to agree hobbled the Iraqi government and prevented many needed changes and improvements.

Post–World War II: The Rise of Arab Nationalism in Iraq

During and after World War II, Iraq's political climate continued to worsen. Arab nationalism was on the rise throughout the Middle East, and Iraq became a seething cauldron of resentment against their British overlords and the occupying West. The Arab nationalists were determined to overthrow the British in Iraq, and it became apparent that it was only a matter of time before they achieved their objectives. The British, meanwhile, were coping with the rebuilding of London and recovering from the devastation wrought on Great Britain during World War II.

However, Nuri as-Said's government did not tolerate open expression of the dissension and unrest that permeated the Iraqi countryside. Opposing political parties were not permitted to form until 1946, and as-Said kept a tight rein on their political activities and the press. Government became increasingly less representative and more secret, thus increasing resentment and frustration among the opposition. In response to these tight controls, the dissenters became increasingly revolutionary and militant in their efforts to effect change in Iraq.

The educated populace of Iraq increasingly chafed under the secretive government of Nuri as-Said, the British influence throughout all levels of Iraqi government, and the Saudi-based Hashemite monarchy. Additionally, Arab nationalism was becoming increasingly attractive to the Iraqi elite. After their failed coup during the war, the Iraqi military suffered the mistrust and maltreatment of the government. The Free Officers movement sought complete Iraqi independence. Finally, tensions between the majority Shiites and the dominant minority Sunnis were still high.

In addition, the Iraqi economy spiraled into a recession and then a depression following World War II. Inflation was rampant, but the Iraqi standard of living was dropping. As stated before, the British-supported as-Said and the Arab nationalist regent were in perpetual opposition to each other. Instead of cooperating to improve the quality of life among the Iraqi citizens, the regent and as-Said could not agree on a cohesive economic policy, infrastructure improvements, and other needed internal initiatives. The Iraqi economy was chiefly an export economy and was based on providing oil and food to the British. In turn, the British did not pay full market value for the goods they imported, further crippling the Iraqi economy. In years of drought or other poor crop yields, this meant deprivation and even starvation for the Iraqi people.

The oil industry continued to dominate the Iraqi economy but was overseen by a conglomerate of British, French, and American interests. The Iraqi Petroleum Company was controlled by outsiders and, to the Iraqis, was just another example of economic imperialism and Western colonialism. To further compound the issue, although Iraqi oil revenues climbed dramatically, corrupt government officials retained the majority of the increased revenue, thus extending the hardships of the Iraqi people.

After the conclusion of World War II, the United States became increasingly involved in Iraqi affairs, especially the Iraqi oil industry. Additionally, as part of the Eisenhower Doctrine, the United States provided military aid to Iraq for resisting communism and containing the Soviet Union. Although there were active communist sympathizers in Iraq during the 1950s, the Arab nationalists continued to hold power throughout Iraq, and that was enough for Iraq to receive aid under the Eisenhower Doctrine.

Iraq, sponsored by the British, became a member of the United Nations in 1945. The British and the United States created a coalition of Arab countries called the Arab League in 1946. Members included Jordan, Lebanon, Saudi Arabia, Yemen, Syria, Egypt, and Iraq. The purpose of the Arab League was to promote containment of the Soviet Union during the Cold War. By the 1950s, the Arab League was staunchly pan-Arabic and worked toward creation of a unified Arab state and anti-Israeli policies. Both Iraq and Egypt struggled to dominate the Arabic world throughout the late 1940s and into the 1950s.

In 1948, the British and the Iraqis signed a new treaty, detailing their new relationship in the post–World War II era. Called the Portsmouth Treaty, the British once again took control of Iraqi foreign affairs, especially on the notion of Iraqi defense and sovereignty. The Arab nationalists in Iraq were incensed by this affront to the sovereignty of Iraq and led the Wathbah Rebellion later that year.

The Wathbah Rebellion was partly in response to the devastating Portsmouth Treaty but was also caused by Iraq's deepening economic issues. Iraq's involvement in the Israel War[1] (sometimes called the Israeli War of Independence) caused further economic devastation throughout Iraq because oil exports out of the Haifa pipeline were choked off during the 1948–1949 war. Nearly half the remaining oil production went to the Iraqi army to support the war effort. This corresponding drop in oil revenue caused massive inflation and famine throughout Iraq, increasing civil unrest and resentment. In many ways, the Portsmouth Treaty was the match to the powder keg that Iraq became during the Israel War.

As-Said and the British were able to defeat the Wathbah Rebellion, but the Arab nationalists were gaining strength and popularity throughout Iraq. As a concession to help put down the Wathbah Rebellion, as-Said agreed to the Arab nationalist demand to renounce the Portsmouth Treaty. The repudiation of the Portsmouth Treaty was a significant, crucial victory for the Iraqi and Arab nationalists because it represented the first time that the Iraqis were able to win concessions from the British. British control was slipping, and the pro-British as-Said government was failing throughout Iraq.

On January 17, 1953, the first free general direct elections took place in Iraq, in accordance with the Iraqi constitution. The newly elected government was also pro-British and therefore was directly opposed by the Arab nationalists in Iraq. The new parliament was sworn in on January 29, 1953.

Faisal II, having reached his majority age, took the throne on May 2, 1953. However, by 1954, Arab nationalists wrested control of the Iraqi parliament from as-Said and his British cronies. The new parliament rejected the American military aid provided under the Eisenhower Doctrine. As-Said disbanded the parliament on August 4, 1954, and called for reelections. The National Democratic Union, led by Arab nationalists, was soundly defeated, and a pro-Western government again took control of Iraq by September 1954.

After World War II, British influence waned as American influence took on increasing significance in Iraq, much to the resentment of the Iraqi populace and the Arab nationalists. Iraq, with its massive oil deposits and reserves, was attractive economically and was strategically located in relationship to the main Cold War enemy of the West, the Soviet Union.

Three international incidents provoked increased opposition to the Western presence in Iraq. In 1955, Iraq entered into the Baghdad Pact with Iran, Pakistan, and Turkey. The pact was a defense agreement between the four nations and was endorsed by both Great Britain and the United States as an anti-Soviet defense mechanism. Recall that Egypt and Iraq were struggling for dominance in the Arab world at this time. Egypt saw the Baghdad Pact as a provocation. Gamel Abdel Nasser, the Egyptian leader, implored the Iraqi military to overthrow the British-backed Iraqi monarchy. Within three years, the Iraqi military would comply with Nasser's request.

The Iraqi relationship with Egypt further deteriorated when the Egyptians nationalized the Suez Canal, the man-made canal that connects the Indian Ocean and the Mediterranean Sea. In response, the British, French, and Israelis invaded Egypt in 1956. Iraq, as a British ally, had to support the Egyptian invasion. Most Iraqi citizens sympathized with the Egyptians and felt that the Egyptian invasion was just another sign of Western aggression and dominance. To avert a war, the United Nations was able to forge an agreement, and the British, French, and Israelis withdrew from Egypt. In the end, this invasion of Egypt fanned the fires of Arab and Iraqi nationalism.

As stated before, Egypt and Iraq were locked in a struggle for dominance over the Arab world. Nasser, the Egyptian leader, supported the concept of a United Arab Republic (UAR), a pan-Arabic notion of a unified Arab state in the Middle East. Nasser positioned Egypt as the leader of the UAR. Only Syria, Yemen, and Egypt ever joined the UAR, and Syria and Yemen withdrew by the early 1960s.

Iraqi leadership had no interest in uniting with Egypt and instead proposed their own pan-Arab state called the Arab Union (AU). Jordan joined Iraq as part of the AU, and Nuri as-Said was named the head of the AU. The Iraqi parliament ratified this decision in May 1958. Great Britain and the United States openly supported the AU, which basically doomed it from the start. Dissenters in Iraq and in other Arabic countries viewed the AU as just another tool of the Western overlords. Nasser of Egypt seized on this sentiment and insisted that the AU was really just an attempt to defeat the UAR.

He also encouraged the Iraqi people and military to overthrow the Western-backed Iraqi government. This time, they would listen.

THE REVOLUTION OF 1958

The Free Officers, a secret military group supporting Arab nationalism led by General Abduel Karim Quasim, overthrew the monarchy on July 14, 1958. This date is still celebrated in Iraq as Iraqi Independence Day. King Faisal II, the regent Abd al Ilah, and Prime Minister Nuri as-Said were executed. The Free Officers were considered heroes throughout much of the populace; however, the Sunni Free Officers themselves did little to reach out to the non-Sunni population. The following day, the Free Officers abolished the AU and announced their intention to join the Egyptian-led UAR. They also renamed the country the Republic of Iraq, a name by which it is still known today.

The leaders of the Free Officers were Abdel-Karin Quasim (Kassem) and Abd al-Salam Arif (Araf). After the rebellion, Quasim was installed as prime minister. By March 1959, they withdrew from the Baghdad Pact and created alliances with communist and socialist countries, including Russia. Because of their agreement with Russia, Quasim's government was forced to allow the formation of the Iraqi Communist Party, Quasim and Arif's ideological opposite. They also withdrew from the sterling bloc, which meant that Iraqi currency was no longer tied to the pound sterling.

Quasim's heritage is worth noting. He was of Sunni and Shiite descent, perhaps making him an ideal ruler to unite the two Islamic factions. Throughout his reign as prime minister, he struggled to pacify both groups, with limited success. Additionally, he was forced to contend with the opposing socialist and Arab nationalists groups throughout his tenure.

In 1960, the British withdrew from Kuwait and declared it an independent state. Quasim promptly invaded Kuwait. Recall that, to the Iraqi worldview, Kuwait was historically part of the Ottoman Basra *vilayet* and was erroneously divided from Iraq after World War I. Kuwait possessed significant oil reserves and a considerable coastline, which were no doubt also attractive to the Iraqis. With the support of the United Nations and the Arab League, the British defended their former protectorate by sending troops into Kuwait. The Iraqis withdrew and ended diplomatic relations with most of their Arab neighbors.

With the regime distracted by the Kuwait conflict, the Iraqi Kurds made a bold bid for freedom from the Iraqi state. Quasim attempted to end the uprising but was ultimately drawn into a protracted conflict with the Kurds, further weakening the shaky regime.

Even after the Free Officers' initial goals of ridding Iraq of British influence and the British-installed monarchy had been achieved, divisions remained. The two main divisions were between the Arab nationalists, who wanted to reach out to the other Arab nations, and the Iraqi nationalists, who were aligned with the communists. The country descended into power struggles, leading to the rise of the Ba'athists.

In the late 1940s, Michel Aflaq and Salah ad-Din al-Bitar founded the Ba'ath Party in Syria. In Arabic, "Ba'ath" means both "rebirth" and "insurrection." The Ba'ath Party motto was "One Arab nation with an eternal mission." They did not recognize the boundaries imposed on the Arab world after the conclusion of World War I. Rather, they viewed the entire region as a collective Arab society. Socialism was the ideological root of the party, although other aims included promotion of pan-Arabism and the defeat of Western imperialism throughout the Middle East. By 1952, the Ba'ath Party was active in Iraq, where they appealed to the young, educated elite. The Ba'athist leader in Iraq was Fu'ad ar Rikabi. Interestingly, Rikabi was a Shiite, but wealthy, educated Sunnis soon overtook the Ba'ath Party. One Ba'athist in particular stood out: Saddam Hussein.

NOTE

1. The Israel War (or the Israeli War of Independence) was between the newly formed Israel and Iraq, Syria, Jordan, Egypt, and Palestine. By 1949, Israeli air supremacy forced the Arab nations to negotiate peace with the new nation of Israel.

8

A Decade of Revolutions and the Rise of Saddam

Iraq endured a decade of revolutions, rebellions, and power shifts between the Revolution of 1958 and the rise to power of the Ba'athists in 1968. The Ba'athists and the Iraqi Communist Party (ICP) grappled for power over the next 10 years, setting the stage for the 1968 revolution. In July 1968, the Ba'ath Party wrested control of Iraq in the so-called Bloodless Revolution. Al-Bakr was installed as president of Iraq and carried out the consolidation of power with one of his chief deputies, Saddam Hussein. Iraq now controlled its own oil resources, and the oil boom of the early 1970s brought great wealth to Iraq. In 1979, President al-Bakr resigned and granted power to Saddam Hussein.

THE QUASIM ERA AND THE 1963 BA'ATH COUP

After the Revolution of 1958, the leaders of the revolt, Arif and Quasim, supported two opposing ideologies. Arif supported uniting with Egypt as part of the United Arab Republic (UAR), while

Quasim resisted joining the UAR and allied himself closely with the communists. Although Quasim would imprison Arif by the end of 1958, the differences between the two men went beyond the UAR and pan-Arab issues and was really a struggle to create a new national Iraqi identity now that Iraq was free from the bonds of post–World War I imperialism and colonialism.

Over time, the Ba'ath Party took up the causes of pan-Arabism and Arab nationalism as they sought to form a coalition with neighboring Arab nations to challenge the supremacy of the West. The communist parties, whose socialistic ideals were appealing to the long-oppressed Shiites, Kurds, and rural poor, opposed the Ba'athists. Additionally, there were groups working toward democracy and an open society. The National Democratic Union was the most powerful of these groups but never enjoyed the influence of the Ba'athists or the ICP.

In March 1959, Quasim's dominion over Iraq was challenged during the Mosul Revolt. Led by a Free Officer, Abd al-Wahhab al-Shawwaf, the Mosul Revolt was still in its planning stages when Quasim and the communists organized a large communist rally for the Peace Partisans. Fighting broke out on the third day, and many well-known, influential Mosul families and nationalists were killed. Al-Shawwaf's allies did not come to his aid, and he died in the bombing raids that Quasim dispatched to the city. The Kurds then attacked Mosul, and chaos ensued. Although Quasim was ultimately able to put down the revolt, execute the rebel leaders, and crack down on the ICP, the Mosul Revolt showcased the deep divides that existed throughout Iraq.

The Mosul Revolt and the following uprisings in Kirkuk inspired several Ba'ath officers to begin plotting the assassination of Quasim. Despite the fact that Quasim was taking steps to subdue the powerful ICP, the Ba'athists believe that Quasim was too closely allied with the ICP and that the recent revolts showed that he did not have control over the country.

Several young Ba'ath soldiers, including Saddam Hussein, trained for and plotted the assassination. On October 7, 1959, Saddam shot Quasim as he rode through the streets of Baghdad. He was unsuccessful in killing Quasim but did wound him. Saddam was shot in the thigh but managed to flee to Syria. In retaliation, Quasim sought to quash the Ba'ath Party, with public trials for some 78 Ba'ath leaders. For many Iraqis, these public trials were their introduction to Ba'athist ideology and goals and did much to boost their popularity.

Quasim tried to institute considerable social and economic reforms and attempted to revive Iraq's failing economy. He did not possess a unified reform policy but instead worked to disassemble the British-imposed legal and social structures. For many years, one of the most contentious issues was that Iraqi oil revenues flowed into British coffers rather than the Iraqi treasury (less than 5 percent of oil revenues stayed in Iraq). Quasim took steps to retain these oil revenues for the use of the Iraqi government. His government instituted a 50 percent tax on oil profits. Additionally, the Iraqi government helped create a conglomerate of the oil-producing nations of the Middle East. They formed the Organization of Petroleum Exporting Countries (OPEC) in September 1960. United, OPEC could control oil production throughout the region and thus the price of crude oil throughout the world.

Perhaps most significantly, Quasim forced the Iraq Petroleum Company (IPC) to give up about 99.5 percent of its oil territory rights. This move cannily pacified the Arab nationalists because it defied foreign powers and appeased the socialist tendencies of the ICP. However, in reality, it did little to affect IPC's oil production, as its oil-producing facilities were located in the .5 percent that remained privatized.

On February 8, 1963, the Ba'ath Party again staged an uprising against Quasim. This time, they were successful. Quasim was deposed and executed. The Ba'athists ruthlessly murdered their ICP opponents. Again, the Ba'ath Party was motivated by a grand vision of Arab unity, little tempered by the political realities and feasibility of such a solution. The Ba'aths were also motivated by a general disregard for Quasim's socialist relations and policies. Although it is unclear whether the Ba'aths received outside Western assistance to overthrow Quasim, the Ba'ath ideology was certainly more aligned with the Western worldview and anti-Soviet Cold War stance.

Presumably to give the new Ba'athist government legitimacy and to promote good relations with the other Arab nations, General Abd al-Salam Arif, Quasim's former ally during the Revolution of 1958, was appointed to the post of president under the Ba'athists but was in actuality far more moderate than his Ba'athist supporters. Real government power was seated in the National Council of the Revolutionary Command. Fissures soon developed between the older, military men and the civilian ideologues.

In addition, ongoing issues with the Ba'athists' Kurdish allies presented difficulty. From 1961, the Kurds, led by Mustafa al-Barzini, head of the Kurdish Democratic Party, challenged Quasim's government control over the northern Kurdish areas. The Kurds sought their autonomy and believed that the Ba'athists would allow them free rule and virtual independence from the Iraqi state in exchange for Kurdish assistance during the 1963 coup. Like the British before them, the Ba'athists broke their promises to the Kurds, who promptly rose up against them. Although Quasim was able to defeat the Kurds, his protracted battles with them further weakened his shaky hold on power.

However, the Ba'ath Party, like the Free Officers of 1958, did not have a vision beyond deposing Quasim and unifying with other Arab nations. After the 1963 coup, they were fragmented and quarreled among themselves. Ideologically, they were akin to Nasser of Egypt but were not adept at promoting support within Iraq for their pan-Arab goals. The Ba'ath Party did not attempt to integrate former Quasim supporters into a new government or a unified political structure. Instead, the Ba'athists sought to enforce their power by brute force and enjoyed killing sprees and purging rampages throughout Iraq, especially targeting their former opponents, the ICP, at least in part in revenge for the torment of Ba'athists during the Quasim regime. Therefore, the Ba'aths were not able to hold power for long and were pushed out of power by November 1963 by General Abd al-Salam Arif, Quasim's former ally during the Revolution of 1958.

The Arif Regime (1963–1968)

On November 18, 1963, Arif took control of the government and proclaimed himself president and commander in chief. He then set about removing the remaining Ba'athists from power. Arif was greatly influenced by the Egyptian Nasser's concept of Arab nationalism and unity. Many Iraqi nationalists saw Arif's overtures to Nasser as too great a concession to Egyptian supremacy in the Arab world. Although most Iraqi nationalists were pan-Arabic, they wanted Iraq to be the dominant Arab nation. Arif was able to stabilize Iraq and give the country some much needed rest after the turbulence of recent years. Arif was able to strike a needed balance between the ICP's socialist ideals and the Ba'athists' ruthless determination for Arab unity.

In May 1964, Arif introduced a new Iraqi provisional constitution that strove to meld all the disparate elements of Iraqi society. Later

that same year, the Arif government set forward a set of nationalization laws that gave the state ownership of most of Iraqi industries.
Arif liberalized and opened the government of Iraq. He even engineered a 1964 Kurdish cease-fire and brokered a June 1966 accord
with Barzani and the Kurdish Democratic Party. Arif also created
the Iraq National Oil Company to compete with the IPC.

General Abd al-Salam Arif died in a sandstorm-caused helicopter
crash in April 1966. His prime minister, Abd al Rahman al-Bazzaz,
stepped in as interim president, but the cabinet elected Arif's brother,
Abd al-Rahman Arif. By June 1966, the Iraqi military attempted
another coup but was ultimately unsuccessful. By the spring of 1967,
Arif occupied not only the office of president but also that of prime
minister. Although the second Arif tried, he could not prevent the
government that his brother had worked so hard to create from
unraveling.

The final blow to the second Arif regime was Iraq's involvement
in the 1967 Arab–Israeli war. Partially brought about by the new
Ba'athist regime in Syria, the Syrians led a loose Arab coalition
to oppose Israel. Although many in Iraq were anti-Israeli, Iraq's
participation in the war was based more on concessions to their
neighbors than on true animus. The Iraqi military participation
was minimal, but nonetheless Arif's government was forced to
concede defeat along with the other Arab governments, doing little
to endear Arif and his cronies to the local populace. Arif's defeat in
the Arab–Israeli war made his government appear weak, perhaps
inviting the 1968 Ba'athist coup.

THE SECOND BA'ATHIST COUP

On July 17, 1968, the Ba'athists were once again able to take power.
The Ba'athists were aligned with some of Arif's disenchanted inner
circle, which assisted them during the uprising. A non-Ba'athist
group, the Arab Revolutionary Movement, led by military leaders,
seized the government without a shot being fired. For this reason, the
1968 revolution is occasionally referred to as the "white," or "bloodless," revolution. However, the Arab Revolutionary Movement
quickly learned that seizing power is much easier than keeping
power when the Ba'athists took over their coup and ousted them
within two weeks.

General Ahmed Hussein al-Bakr, a relative of Saddam Hussein,
led the Ba'athist government. Al-Bakr was a member of the Free

Officers and believed in the Soviet style of socialist government, which was akin to a dictatorship. Centralization and nationalization were decreed from the top rather than as a democratic process. In al-Bakr's regime, like the Soviet Union, dissenters were harshly punished and, generally, summarily executed.

By the end of 1968, al-Bakr's government issued an interim constitution, declared Islam the state religion, and granted the Revolutionary Command Council (RCC) supreme authority over all Iraq. The Iraqi president also served as the leader of the RCC and the commander in chief of the military. In significant contrast to their earlier attempts to seize power, the Ba'athists retained power among themselves. They nationalized the military and, because the president was required to ratify any regional appointee to the RCC, guaranteed a one-party state. Additionally, most of the top Ba'athists were from the Tikrit region and therefore possessed tribal as well as ideological bonds.

Socialism did not translate well to an underindustrialized nation, as Iraq was in the late 1960s. At that time, Iraq was mostly an agricultural society. The oil industry was booming and had been since before World War II, but most people were involved in agrarian pursuits rather than industrial efforts. Heavy investment by the state, as called for in socialist theory, minimized and retarded private investment. This process started with the first Arif administration, when Arif nationalized most of the industries in Iraq, and was further emphasized when the Ba'athists came to power. By the 1970s, the Ba'athist government controlled nearly all Iraqi industries, and most continued to function by relying on Iraq's oil revenues. By 1975, all of Iraq's oil industry was controlled by the government.

After the bloodless coup of 1968, the Ba'athists began a reign of terror in Iraq, striking down any real or perceived opponents through the widespread use of sham trials, executions, and "disappearances." Additionally, the Ba'athists aligned themselves with the Soviet Union against the United States and Great Britain during the Cold War. The Ba'athists were also opposed to Israel—viewing it as an affront to Arab unity and nationalism. Additionally, they continued Iraq's long history of opposing the Persian led Iranians, leading to war in the 1980s.

Al-Bakr and the Ba'athists also negotiated a peace treaty with the Kurds. They agreed to a manifesto that recognized Kurdish autonomy. Although the interim constitution declared that no part of Iraq could break away (thereby dashing the Kurds' hopes for an independent country), the constitution did recognize the Kurds as a separate and distinct nationality, a major victory for the long-suffering Kurds.

In the early 1970s, Iraq again participated in an Arab–Israeli conflict. On October 6, 1973, a coalition of Iraq, Syria, Egypt, and Jordan attacked Israel. Although the United States and the Soviet Union were able to broker a cease-fire, Iraq continued fighting until 1974. Following the 1973 war with Israel, oil prices rose dramatically, bringing enormous wealth and economic power to Iraq and the rest of the Arab world.

THE RISE TO POWER OF SADDAM HUSSEIN

Although al-Bakr was nominally the head of state in Iraq, Saddam Hussein increasingly gained power and influence behind the scenes. Because Saddam Hussein is a significant and crucial figure in Iraq's modern history, let us pause here for an introduction to Saddam Hussein.

Born in late April 1937 (scholars differ on the date) to a poor widowed peasant woman in al-Awja, near the northern Iraqi village of Tikrit, Saddam's name means "one who confronts." Later stories contend that his Tikriti family claims descent from Abi Taleb, the fourth Muslim caliph, although this genealogy is difficult to prove conclusively after more than 1,000 years. Saddam himself was part of the al-Khattab clan and bears the tridot tattoo of his tribe on his right hand. As according to custom, his mother married his late father's brother, and they moved to a small, impoverished town north of Tikrit. Scholars have made much of his stepfather's harsh cruelty and Saddam's removal from Tikrit. Certainly, the harshness of his early years contributed to his extraordinary capacity for cruelty and cunning that marked his long reign.

In 1947, when Saddam was 10 years old, he ran away from his stepfather's home and returned to Tikrit. There he attended school and lived under the guardianship of his maternal uncle, Khair Allah Talfah. Talfah was a devout Sunni and passed this devotion on to his young nephew. Talfah had been imprisoned for his participation in the 1941 Rashid Ali rebellion against the British. It is probable that Saddam developed his anti-British, anti-Semitic, and Arab nationalist preferences during his uncle's guardianship. In the mid-1950s, Talfah became the governor of Baghdad, and this made up Saddam's early introduction to national politics and power. Saddam attended secondary school in Baghdad and joined the Ba'ath Party in 1957, no doubt attracted by its pan-Arabism and socialist ideals.

Saddam was imprisoned for six months with his uncle, allegedly for a political murder in Tikrit. Supposedly, he murdered a prominent ICP member who was also his brother-in-law. As previously discussed, Saddam was part of the Ba'ath Party's 1959 attempted assassination of Quasim. Later legend claims that Saddam himself fired the shot that wounded Quasim. Saddam was wounded in the leg during the attempt and took refuge in Syria. Some stories claim that he fled disguised as a woman. Significantly, Saddam proved himself a loyal Ba'athist during the assassination attempt and cemented his choice position in the party. In absentia, he was sentenced to death in Iraq for his part in the assassination attempt on Quasim.

Eventually, he made his way to Egypt, where he met with Nasser. At that time, Nasser was the model Arab statesman, promoting pan-Arabism, anti-Zionism, and anti-Westernism, and Saddam idolized him. No doubt, Saddam's meeting with his idol helped solidify Saddam's own political aspirations. While in Egypt, Saddam married his cousin, Sajida Talfah. They had five children together, two sons and three daughters. Saddam's sons, Uday and Qusay, would later help their father terrorize and control his citizens. While in Egypt, Saddam continued his political activities and studied law at the University of Cairo.

On Arif's ascension to power, Saddam returned to Iraq in February 1963 to assist the short-lived Ba'athist regime. He oversaw an Iraqi prison and torture chamber. After Arif managed to wrest power from the Ba'athists in November 1963, Saddam continued working to gain power for the Ba'athists in Iraq. He helped create a secret Iraqi police force and intelligence agency. Saddam then went to Syria to coordinate Ba'ath Party planning with party founder Michael Aflaq. He was part of the 1965 attempted coup against the Arif regime and once again was forced to flee the country. Saddam played a major role in the 1968 coup that finally secured Ba'athist power in Iraq.

Officially, Saddam served as vice president of the RCC in al-Bakr's government. It is important to note that prominent men from Tikrit held most of the top positions in the Ba'ath Party and the al-Bakr government. Those holding the three top positions— Saddam, al-Bakr, and Hammad Shihab—were blood relatives. This loyalty to Tikrit natives would become a distinguishing characteristic of Saddam's reign and helped him hold power for so long.

Behind the scenes, he was viewed as a political asset to the Ba'ath Party. Initially at least, his rural and tribal background helped the more urban, elite, intellectual Ba'athists appeal to the Iraqi tribes. He negotiated the 1970 peace treaty with the Kurds and worked to improve relations with the Soviet Union. Behind the scenes, Saddam was in charge of the feared secret police and security force, funded by the vast oil profits of the early 1970s, and did much to secure al-Bakr's power in Iraq. Saddam and al-Bakr formed an effective government team. Al-Bakr possessed significant military experience and prestige. Saddam was considerably younger than al-Bakr and did not have any military experience, a distinct disadvantage in a military-based government. Saddam became al-Bakr's power behind the throne who executed secret plots on his behalf.

Neither Saddam nor al-Bakr was a visionary ideologue. Instead, Saddam ruled on the basis of tribal customs and mores. In many ways, Saddam's rule over Iraq was akin more to a patriarchal tribal sheik than to a state leader. Throughout his political career, he relied on kinship ties and clan loyalty rather than devotion to any one political concept or theory.

Al-Bakr and Saddam were able to foil a Nasser-backed coup in September 1968 and launched a series of massive purges to help consolidate their power. Anyone who was perceived as challenging their authority was stripped of all possessions and tossed out of the Ba'ath Party. Many were imprisoned, tortured, and eventually murdered. Entire families were wiped out so that no remaining family members would be able to exact revenge for those killed. These bloody purges gave rise to a reign of terror throughout Iraq. Saddam also established a Ba'ath militia that later would become his fanatically loyal Republican Guard. By the time Saddam took power in 1979, the Republican Guard had swelled to more than 50,000 members.

By the early 1970s, the treaty that Saddam had managed to negotiate with the Kurds was collapsing. In the treaty, the Kurds were allowed to develop a militia called the Pesh Merga. The 1970 treaty did not specify land boundaries of Kurdish autonomy, and this frustrated the Kurds. By 1973, the Kurds were seriously challenging Ba'ath authority and control. Saddam and the Ba'athists attempted to assassinate the Kurdish leader and his son. When the plot failed, Saddam was able to align with the Soviet Union for assistance to keep the rebellious Kurds in line. In turn, the Kurds sought aid from the Iranians. Recall that the Kurds' ethnic heritage is much more akin to the Iranians, who are of Persian descent, than the Iraqis, who are of Arab descent. The Kurds also allied with the United States, which was still interested in containing communism during the height of the Cold War. The Kurds also received aid from Syria and from Israel.

Saddam was instrumental in negotiating the Algiers Agreement with Iran to cease its aid and support to the Kurds. As part of the agreement, the Iraqis and the Iranians agreed to waterway rights for the Shatt-al-Arab River. As we will see in the next chapter, this waterway would be crucial in the development of the Iran–Iraq War of the 1980s.

Following the Algiers Agreement, Iraqi military and the Pesh Merga fought several fierce battles. Many Kurdish villages were destroyed and the Kurds were forced to flee their homeland. Saddam sent Arab settlers into the traditional Kurdish territories. The Kurdish Democratic Party lost legitimacy with the Kurds, and a rival party, the Patriotic Union of Kurdistan, developed in 1975. The Kurdish Democratic Party and the Patriotic Union of Kurdistan now fought each other rather than the Iraqi troops.

Al-Bakr's government created a number of significant economic reforms. It instituted an industrial modernization program in 1976, created land reform programs that distributed ownership of farmland to rural owners, and worked hard to improve the infrastructure of Iraq. These popular reforms did much to help the Iraqis accept their new Ba'athist leadership.

When President Anwar Sadat of Egypt signed the Camp David Accords in 1978, the Arab world denounced Egypt. To the Arab mind-set, Egypt's formal recognition of Israel and the right of the Zionist state to exist was tantamount to treason. Egypt, for so long the leader of the Arab world, was now a pariah. Saddam Hussein led an Arab summit in Baghdad and joined in denouncing Egypt and the Camp David Accords. Iraq was now recognized as a leader in the Arab world, and Saddam was ready to take the leadership role.

On July 16, 1979, al-Bakr was in poor health and resigned from politics. Some stories hold that Saddam arrested him. Al-Bakr named Saddam as his successor and vested him with executive power. Regardless of how al-Bakr's resignation took place, Saddam stood ready to step into the power vacuum. Saddam would rule Iraq through the Iran–Iraq War, two Gulf wars, and 10 years of UN sanctions before the United States would oust him from power in 2003.

9

A Decade of Wars: The Iran–Iraq War and Gulf War I

We have seen how Saddam Hussein managed to consolidate the Ba'athist hold on power and take control in 1979. In 1980, the eight-year Iran–Iraq War broke out, partially over border disputes but also based on differences between Iran's Islamic religious–based state and Iraq's more secular Ba'athist government. After the cease-fire between Iraq and Iran in 1988, Saddam Hussein turned his attention to Kuwait.

The southern division between Iraq and Kuwait was artificially imposed during the British Mandate but was never accepted by Iraqi nationalists. After the Iran–Iraq War ended, Iraq needed to keep oil prices high to rebuild its war-torn country. Kuwait increased its oil production, thereby driving prices lower. In retaliation, Saddam Hussein invaded Kuwait in August 1990. In January 1991, the United States bombarded Iraq and Kuwait, leading to the withdrawal of Iraqi troops. Iraq then endured 13 years of UN sanctions until Gulf War II ended in 2003.

THE IRAN–IRAQ WAR

After Saddam Hussein took power in 1979, he moved quickly to eliminate any potential competition or perceived enemies. President al-Bakr resigned on July 18, 1979. Within days, Saddam convened a meeting of the Revolutionary Command Council (RCC) and other senior officials. As the videotape that he later distributed throughout Iraq shows, Saddam announced that he was assuming power in response to a Syrian plot to overthrow the Iraqi government. Muhya al-Din Abd al-Hussein, a member of the RCC, was forced to make a public confession of the supposed Syrian plot and named nearly 70 RCC and government officials as conspirators in the plot. Many of them were arrested on the spot. Sham trials were conducted, and 22 of the accused were executed. Most of the rest were given lengthy prison terms. With this public spectacle, Saddam made it clear that he was in charge and perfectly willing to go to extraordinary lengths to achieve his goals and keep his hold on power.

Recall that Saddam was instrumental in negotiating the Algiers Agreement with Iran to cease its aid and support to the Kurds in 1975. Prior to the Algiers Agreement, a 1937 treaty negotiated by the British governed the Shatt-al-Arab waterway. Under the 1937 treaty, Iraq held control over the channel. In return for Iraqi maintenance to allow ships to navigate the waterway, Iran was required to pay fees for usage of the Shatt-al-Arab. Under the terms of the 1937 treaty, the international border of the Shatt-al-Arab coincided with the Iranian coastline.

After the British withdrew from the region, Iran began to violate the terms of the 1937 treaty. By 1971, Iran controlled several key Gulf islands of the United Arab Emirates that lay along the Shatt-al-Arab waterway. To Iraq, this represented a challenge to its oil shipments and a threat to control of the valuable Strait of Hormuz, which separates the Persian Gulf from the Indian Ocean.

In the Algiers Agreement, Saddam and the shah of Iran agreed to move the boundary of the Shatt-al-Arab into the middle of the waterway (from the coastline of Iran) in exchange for the Iranians ceasing their military and arms assistance to the rebellious Kurds of northern Iraq. After the 1975 agreement, the historically rocky relationship between Iraq and Iran became relatively civil. Saddam even assisted the shah by deporting a troublesome Shiite cleric, the Ayatollah Khomeini.

Ruhollah Khomeini was a learned Shiite cleric who earned the title "Ayatollah" in 1950. Roughly akin to a bishop in the Catholic hierarchy, an ayatollah is considered a significant religious leader among the Shiites Muslims. Khomeini was very critical of the secular governments of the Iranian shah and Iraq's Ba'athists. In 1978, Saddam deported Khomeini from the Shiite holy city of An-Najaf in Iraq. Khomeini spent a year in Paris before returning to Iran during the Iranian Islamic Revolution of 1979.

Khomeini attained power in Iran in February 1979 and proclaimed that henceforth Iran would be known as the Islamic Republic of Iran. As ayatollah, Khomeini held considerable influence over Shiite Muslims around the world, including in Iraq. Khomeini made no secret of the fact that he loathed the man who had deported him less than year earlier and openly called for the Iraqi Shiites to overthrow the regime. Understandably, Saddam was also less than delighted that the man he had summarily deported less than a year previously now controlled not only the enemy Iranians but also the majority of his own people. He feared that Khomeini would resume arms shipments to the rebellious Kurds and that the Iraqi Shiites would support an Iranian coup against him. Saddam wanted Iraq to be the unquestioned leader of the Arab world and viewed Khomeini as a threat to this supremacy, especially among Iraq's majority Shiite Muslims.

He also believed, incorrectly, that the revolution had weakened Iraq's former enemy and that Iran was ripe for an Iraqi coup and control. Additionally, Saddam believed that he would be able to gain the support of the Arab population in the Iranian region of Khuzestan (which the Iraqis called Arabistan) and therefore gain Iraqi control over their rich oil fields.

Khomeini wanted to promote an Iranian style theocracy throughout the Middle East, a concept that was popular among Shiite Muslims around the world, including in Iraq. In addition, Iraq controlled the two holiest sites in Shiite Islam, An-Najaf and Karbala, where Ali's sons were martyred.

In April 1980, the Shiite group al-Da'wah attempted to assassinate two of Saddam's cabinet members. Al-Da'wah wanted to create an Iraqi fundamentalist Shiite state modeled on Iran. Saddam executed their leader, Baqir as Sadier, but took the opportunity to deport thousands of Shiites to Iran. He also placed the blame for the assassination attempts squarely on Khomeini.

Saddam renounced the Algiers Agreement in September 1980 and asserted full Iraqi control over the Shatt-al-Arab waterway, much to the dismay of the Iranians. Fighting broke out by September 21, 1980, and Iraq sent troops to invade Iran. Saddam believed that he would easily defeat the Iranians, as he possessed significant troves of Soviet weapons and tanks as well as a fanatically trained army.

The Iranian army leadership was decimated during the 1979 revolution, although most foot soldiers were spared the bloodletting. Most of the Iranian officers were Shiite clerics with little or no military experience. Saddam assumed, incorrectly, that the military would be in complete disarray following the recent Iranian revolution and wished to take advantage of this perceived weakness. Their equipment was old and no match for Saddam's Soviet-supplied abundance of weapons. However, Iran did possess air superiority, as it had several American jets that it had just put to good use fending off the attempted American hostage rescue attempt in April 1980. Iran also had a considerably greater population that it could draw from to support a protracted conflict.

The Iranians launched several successful air strikes against the Iraqis, but initially Saddam gained significant ground. Saddam took the Arab-controlled oil-rich area of Khuzestan as well as several significant Iranian roads and waterways. Iran utilized its own "republican guard," called the Pasdaran, and the Basij fighters, a group of devout Shiites who were willing to be martyred in battle.

Syria assisted Iran by cutting off the Iraqi oil pipeline, choking the Iraqis economically. Saddam offered a peace treaty to the Iranians but was flatly rejected. By January 1981, the Iranians became the aggressor. Despite the incompetence of the Iranian president and commander, BaniSadir, the Iranians were able to make significant progress by the end of 1981. They forced the Iraqis to retreat from the Iranian-occupied territory, and the Iranian air force was able to effectively target all of Iraq.

By March 1982, the Iranians were able to force the Iraqis into retreat. In June 1982, Saddam again sought to negotiate a peace treaty with Khomeini but was rebuffed. Instead, the Iranians attacked Basra and continued on the offensive despite enormous Iranian casualties. The Iranians utilized a tactic termed the "human wave" in which groups of Basij ran at the enemy or through minefields until reaching the enemy line where hand-to-hand combat would break out. This tactic, while effective, resulted in heavy losses for the Iranians, many of them children.

By 1984, Iraq was on the defensive and was unable to muster an effective counterattack. Saddam began using chemical weapons, such as mustard gas and nerve gas, against the Iranians. In April 1984, Saddam again offered an olive branch to Khomeini but was refused. The war devolved into a war of attrition, with each side sustaining massive casualties. A single battle in late February 1984 alone cost more than 25,000 lives. The Iranians, sustained by their religious fervor, were able to stomach a profound loss of life to support their cause. The Iraqis, however, were not.

In what would later become known as the Iran-Contra Affair, the United States began supplying Iran with weapons in 1985. Recall that Iraq was using Soviet-supplied weaponry and that, as this was still during the Cold War, the United States supported Iran as part of a Soviet containment policy. By 1987, the United States became more concerned about the Basra region (which contains the oil export ports of Iraq) becoming an Iranian theocracy and then began supporting Iraq with military aid.

By February 1986, the Iranians controlled the critical Iraqi port of al-Faw, where Iraqi oil was shipped. By the time the Iraqis were able to retake al-Faw in 1988, the oil production facilities were destroyed. In January 1987, Iran launched another aggressive strike against Basra but called off the strike in late February 1987. No significant gains were achieved despite the continued heavy casualties on both sides.

During the 1986 "tanker war," when both Iraq and Iran indiscriminately attacked and sank ships throughout the Persian Gulf, several Kuwaiti tankers were sunk. The interference with shipping—and therefore Middle Eastern oil production—greatly concerned the West. The United States and the Soviet Union sent tankers into the region. In May 1987, the Iraqis hit the USS *Stark* with two Exocet missiles and killed nearly 40 U.S. naval officers.

Although Iraq did apologize, the United States sponsored UN Security Council Resolution 598, which demanded that Iran and Iraq cease hostilities. Resolution 598 also stated that Iran and Iraq would observe prewar boundaries and provided for UN aid to assist in rebuilding and war recovery efforts. The United States and the UN hoped that this would result in increased oil production and therefore lower oil prices. Khomeini refused to acknowledge Resolution 598 and sought to have Iraq punished for its aggression in starting the war.

In 1988, during the so-called War of the Cities, Iran attacked Baghdad with multiple missile launches. Iraq responded in kind, and Iran feared the Iraqis would launch chemical warheads next. Additionally, the Iraqi army was now better equipped than the Iranians (thanks to the Americans following the Iran-Contra Affair) and was able to retake al-Faw in early 1988. After eight years of war, Iran and Iraq finally agreed and accepted Resolution 598 in the summer of 1988.

An uneasy peace now existed between the historic opponents, but the underlying tensions that caused the war still existed. Iraq supported a secular form of government in comparison with the theocratic Iranian model. The Iraqi Shiites still viewed Khomeini as a religious and spiritual leader. The Kurds were still restless and sought their own homeland. Despite the devastating human and economic consequences of their eight-year struggle, nothing had truly changed between Iran and Iraq.

During the war, Iran lost nearly 1 million people, while Iraq lost nearly 400,000. Iraq now possessed the premier Arab military, with a well-equipped, highly trained fighting force of more than 1 million men. Iraq also emerged from the war with massive national debt, taken on to support the eight years of fighting. Iraq oil revenues were very low because of the disruption of oil production throughout the war.

Iraq After the Iran–Iraq War

Iraq emerged from the war with a massive national debt. Its biggest creditor was the tiny nation of Kuwait, its southern neighbor. Saddam now had a massive military to support and virtually no oil revenue to help him. Additionally, the prewar prosperity that Iraq enjoyed was gone, leaving restless, hungry, frustrated citizens throughout Iraq. Despite his continued use of terror tactics, Saddam's hold on power was shaken by the drastic decline in the Iraqi quality of life.

Saddam's hopes for his coveted leadership position in the Arab world were also fading. Rather than being the regional superpower, Iraq was now dependent on the neighboring Arab states. The Iran–Iraq War did improve Iraq's relationship with the West, most notably (and perhaps ironically) the United States, which sought to contain a common enemy in Iran. Iraq also built a better relationship with France during this time. The Iraq–Soviet relationship cooled considerably during this time, mostly because of the Soviet Union's internal problems and coming systemic collapse.

Although the lengthy, devastating war did promote cohesion between the Iraqi Sunni population, the Shiites and the Kurds were increasingly disenfranchised. As a whole, the Iraqi Shiites did not oppose Iraq and side with Iran, as Saddam feared at the start of the war. In Iran, the Supreme Assembly for the Islamic Revolution in Iraq (SAIRI) formed to unite the many Shiite groups working toward promoting an Islamic regime in Iraq, but SAIRI was never able to drum up the support of the Iraqi Shiites it needed to have a significant impact. Although Saddam did take steps to integrate the Shiites into his government and promote public works in Shiite areas (at least at the start of the war), he also deported many Iraqi Shiite leaders, and any opposition was met with breathtaking ruthlessness and brutal persecution.

As for the Kurds, initially there was too much infighting among themselves to be much of a threat to destabilizing the Iraqi regime. Most Kurds were ideologically aligned with the Persian Iranians and resisted the Iraqi draft. Throughout 1986 and 1987, the Kurds rebelled throughout the northern Iraqi provinces. In 1987, Ali Hasan al-Majid was appointed governor of the Kurdish region with orders to defeat the insurgency and quell the uprisings.

Al-Majid began a scorched-earth campaign to end the Kurdish insurgency. He and his troops razed towns and villages and forcibly relocated the Kurds. Many Kurds were taken into captivity. Many more were killed and buried in mass graves. Among the Kurds, this brutal campaign is termed the *anfals,* meaning "spoils." The most famous incident was in March 1988 at Halabja, where al-Majid used chemical weapons against the population and murdered some 5,000 Kurds. Al-Majid earned the sobriquet "Chemical Ali" for his brutal actions against the Kurdish population. Although support for Saddam was never strong among the Kurds, after the *anfals* the Kurds despised the despotic regime, creating further instability after the Iran–Iraq War.

From an economic standpoint, during the war the Iranians destroyed the main Iraqi oil export terminals, and Syria cut off the oil pipeline from Iraq to the Mediterranean. The Shatt-al-Arab remained closed to Iraq, so it was impossible to utilize the main port at Basra. The only way for Iraq to now export oil was via land routes through Jordan and Turkey and via a Saudi Arabian pipeline. Yet these methods produced less than two-thirds of prewar oil production. In 1988, the price of crude oil dropped dramatically, lessening Iraq's already reduced revenues to about 25 percent of its prewar levels.

Saddam needed to raise money quickly, and the only way to do that was to increase exports of oil. Unfortunately, Iraq was a member of the Organization of Petroleum Exporting Countries (OPEC) and was bound to comply with the OPEC quotas of oil production to prevent a surplus of oil from flooding the market and suppressing oil prices even further. Even during the war, Saddam attempted to renegotiate Iraq's oil quota but was unsuccessful. By 1989, he was desperate to get the quota increased so that he could begin paying back his multi-billion-dollar debt and was forced to reschedule his debt payments and bargain away much of the oil his country was producing.

GULF WAR I

Understanding the first Gulf War requires a good understanding of the history of relations between Iraq and Kuwait. When the British took control of Mesopotamia during World War I, it declared the emirate of Kuwait an independent and sovereign state. When the San Remo Conference and the Conference of Cairo ended, the tiny nation of Kuwait was created. Although not formally incorporated into the Ottoman Empire, Kuwait was considered part of the Basra *vilayet* during Ottoman times and therefore, to the Iraqi worldview, should be part of Iraq. During the first Gulf War, Saddam argued that the British never defined the border between Kuwait and Iraq and that, therefore, the Kuwait territory was part of Iraq.

Officially, Kuwait became independent on June 19, 1961, after the British withdrew from the region. The al-Saba royal family rules Kuwait. The population of Kuwait is about 1 million natives and about 1.2 million foreign residents. Kuwait is slightly smaller than the U.S. state of New Jersey at just under 18,000 square kilometers. Kuwait's neighbors geographically dwarf it, but Kuwait does possess a lengthy Persian Gulf coastline of 499 kilometers. Kuwait is rich in oil and possesses a strategic deep-sea port on the Persian Gulf.

Despite repeated Iraq's repeated attempts to annex Kuwait, the tiny nation managed to maintain its independence with the aid of powerful friends, such as the United States. After the end of the Iran–Iraq War, Kuwait increased oil production dramatically, which, though not the sole cause, helped cause the 1988 drop in oil prices. In addition, Kuwait possessed functioning oil production facilities, something in short supply in Iraq after the Iran–Iraq War.

Saddam also owed Kuwait money—some $13 billion—and Kuwait would not allow him to continually restructure his debt payments. His army was the premier fighting force in the region and easily dwarfed Kuwait's small force. By invading Kuwait, Saddam could eliminate much of his remaining Iran–Iraq War debt, gain control of Kuwait's oil and oil production facilities, and intimidate his neighbors, especially Saudi Arabia.

Before the invasion, Saddam took steps to ensure that the Iranians would not assist the Kurds in an uprising while the Iraqi army was distracted in the south. In order to do this, he granted the Iranians control of the Shatt-al-Arab waterway—one of the main causes of the bloody, destructive eight-year conflict with the Iranians.

Saddam then proceeded to make his case for invasion of Kuwait. He accused Kuwait of dumping oil on the market to depress world oil prices and of illegally harvesting oil from the joint Iraqi–Kuwaiti Rumalyah oil fields and reasserted the Iraqi belief that Kuwait actually belonged to Iraq. The world's reaction to Saddam's public statements was muted. The Arab nations and the first Bush administration did not forcibly declare their support for Kuwait. In any case, there was no Arab army strong enough to impede Saddam—only the United States posed any threat to Saddam's aggression. Saddam apparently took their silence for assent and invaded Kuwait on August 2, 1990.

Initially, Saddam claimed that his troops invaded Kuwait and took Kuwait City to prevent a rebellion against the emir. On August 9, 1990, he abandoned his claim of suppressing this nonexistent rebellion and annexed Kuwait as the nineteenth Iraqi province. The Kuwaiti military took refuge in Saudi Arabia, and Saddam's troops massed along the Kuwaiti–Saudi Arabian border. Saddam did not invade Saudi Arabia, possibly believing that his annexation of Kuwait would be enough to strike fear throughout the Middle East.

President George H. W. Bush declared that the Iraqi invasion of Kuwait "would not stand" and began formulating a Western–Arab coalition to chase Saddam out of Kuwait. Saudi Arabia granted the United States permission to base troops in its country. Some U.S. troops remain in Saudi Arabia today, an issue that still rankles many Muslims around the world. Egypt, Syria, and Kuwait all joined the U.S.-led coalition in opposition to Saddam. Eventually, it would become a coalition of 38 nations.

After forming this powerful coalition, the United States then worked to get UN support against Saddam. The UN Security Council passed a resolution demanding Saddam retreat from Kuwait. It also set forth economic sanctions against Iraq blocking imports and exports for Iraq, ending Saddam's only remaining revenue source.

Saddam tried to negotiate with the United States and the UN, offering withdrawal for major concessions. To the Western–Arab coalition, giving in to Saddam's requested concessions would reward his aggression. Instead, the United States sent more than 230,000 troops to Saudi Arabia in support of Operation Desert Shield. During the fall of 1991, the United States sent an additional 200,000 troops.

In an attempt to fracture the U.S.-led coalition, Saddam accused President Bush of criminal actions, such as attempting to control Muslim holy sites. Recall that Mecca is located in Saudi Arabia. Saddam further demanded that Bush stand trial in Baghdad for his crimes. When that had no noticeable effect on the coalition, he attempted to make Israel part of the issue.

Saddam wanted to turn the issue into a conflict between Arabs and Israel. The West, especially the United States, was a longtime Israeli ally, while the Arab nations and Israel were in a state of uneasy détente after multiple Arab–Israeli wars. Saddam threatened to attack Israel if the Western–Arab coalition attacked Iraq. He hoped that President Bush's administration would publicly support Israel and therefore turn its Arab allies against the Western–Arab coalition.

In November 1990, the UN Security Council approved a resolution authorizing the Western–Arab coalition to utilized force to evict Iraq from Kuwait. The deadline for Saddam to depart Kuwait was January 15, 1991. The stated goal of the U.S.-led coalition was to force Saddam to leave Kuwait unconditionally.

On January 17, 1991, Operation Desert Shield became Operation Desert Storm, and the U.S.-led coalition began bombing raids inside Kuwait and Iraq, especially in Baghdad. The Western coalition countries were under the command of General Norman Schwarzkopf and the Arab countries under the command of a Saudi Arabian general named Khalid ibn Sultan ibn Abd Al Aziz al Saud. The United States took out Saddam's antiaircraft missile sites early in the war, thus establishing U.S. air supremacy early on.

Saddam began an anti-U.S. public relations campaign. He asserted that the Americans destroyed a Baghdad "baby milk" factory, and when the United States mistakenly bombed the Al-Firdos bunker in Baghdad, Saddam displayed the bodies of the 200 civilians killed on television. Saddam's public relations campaign did have the effect of reducing strategic bombing strikes on Baghdad.

He also launched SCUD missiles, purchased from the Soviet Union during the Iran–Iraq War, at Israel. Saddam desperately wanted to draw Israel into the conflict so as to fracture the U.S.-led coalition. The United States intercepted most of the SCUDs with Patriot missiles. Although some SCUDs did strike Israel, the Israelis showed remarkable forbearance in the face of Saddam's provocation and did not respond militarily. American diplomacy kept Israel out of the war and the Western–Arab alliance intact.

In February 1991, Saddam again attempted to negotiate a conditional withdrawal from Kuwait. The United States rejected his offer and insisted that Saddam unconditionally withdraw from Kuwait. Saddam refused, and after a five-week aerial assault, the United States launched a ground war against his troops.

For more than a month, the United States and the coalition decimated the Iraqi army using B-52 bombers. The ground war became something of a nonevent because the feared Iraqi army gave up without much resistance. On February 24, 1991, the ground war began. The Iraqi army was caught in a vise as coalition troops moved in a "sweeping hook" from the north, south, and west. The Iraqi troops were quickly severed from their communication and supply lines.

On the third day of the ground assault, U.S. forces took Kuwait City. Many of the Iraqi troops were killed or surrendered. Although the Iraqi army was comprised of battle-hardened soldiers, they were accustomed to a protracted, trench warfare. The coalition had speed, mobility, and modern weaponry on its side. They simply overwhelmed an Iraqi army that was unprepared to cope with a radically different type of warfare. As they retreated, they set fire to hundreds of Kuwaiti oil wells, eventually driving up the price of oil in Kuwait.

On February 27, President Bush declared a cease-fire. Saddam Hussein was driven from Kuwait. In light of recent events that are discussed more fully in the next chapter, why didn't Bush and his allies remove Saddam from power? The UN resolutions were intended only to remove Saddam from Kuwait and were silent on removing him from power. In addition, the Western–Arab coalition was fragile. While the Arab nations participating in the coalition did indeed want Saddam removed from Kuwait, they would not have supported an attempt to remove him from Iraq. Bush did not want to take the risk of the coalition fracturing and instead settled on an isolationist policy to try to drive Saddam out of power.

10

Sanctions, Gulf War II, and Iraq Today

After the Gulf War I concluded, Iraq endured 13 years of UN economic sanctions and the requirement for UN weapons inspections. Gulf War II toppled the Hussein regime and led to a U.S.-led presence in Iraq. In January 2005, the first free elections in 50 years took place in Iraq, paving the way for Iraqi self-governance. The history of Iraq is being written today. The future is uncertain, being left to the strength and perseverance of the Iraqi people.

THE AFTERMATH OF GULF WAR I

The U.S.-led coalition negotiated a cease-fire with Tariq Aziz on behalf of Saddam Hussein at the conclusion of Gulf War I. He was required to acknowledge the sovereignty of Kuwait, destroy all his SCUD missiles with a range beyond 150 kilometers, and help pay for rebuilding costs in Kuwait. The terms of the cease-fire said nothing about Saddam's continued sovereignty, and he went back to ruling Iraq much as he had before the war.

The coalition troops did not capture Baghdad or Saddam at the conclusion of Gulf War I. Once the Iraqis were driven from Kuwait, the Western–Arab coalition considered its mission accomplished. The defeated Iraqi army was in disarray and could no longer be used as an effective tool of aggression by Saddam. President George H. W. Bush believed, incorrectly, that Saddam would be vulnerable to attack from within and would probably be overthrown in another military coup. Instead of overthrowing Saddam themselves, the West set about isolating him from his Arab neighbors and the Western world. The West and its Arab allies also feared the total collapse of the Iraqi state and felt that Saddam was a better choice than a fractured Iraq. Iraq's Middle Eastern neighbors did not want an independent Kurdistan or another Shiite controlled theocracy such as Iran.

The United States and its coalition partners turned to the task of rebuilding Kuwait, which suffered from heavy bombing during the war and oil well fires lit by retreating Iraqi troops. The oil fires were eventually quelled after about nine months. However, they caused enormous environmental destruction and devastation and crippled Kuwaiti oil production for years. According to U.S. government estimates, Kuwait spent more than $5 billion to repair oil infrastructure devastated during the Iraqi occupation and ensuing liberation.

In Iraq, the Shiites and the Kurds rose up against Saddam and his regime. However, the Sunni elites in the government and military remained loyal to Saddam and helped him defeat these internal uprisings rather than stage the coup that the West expected. Saddam struck out against the uprisings with brutal force and effectiveness, using chemical weapons and helicopter attacks against the Shiites and the Kurds.

Although the West was unwilling to commit ground troops to assist or defend the Iraqi Kurds and Shiites, the United States, Great Britain, and France did establish and enforce no-fly zones at the thirty-sixth and thirty-third parallels by August 1992. (France ended its protection in 1996.) Iraqi planes were forbidden to enter the no-fly areas. These no-fly zones shielded the northern-based Kurds and the southern-based Shiites from Saddam's aerial assaults but were a major source of conflict in the interim between Gulf War I and Gulf War II.

Over the years between the two Gulf wars, Saddam delighted in provoking Kuwait and the United States by taking forays into the demilitarized zone along the Iraqi–Kuwaiti border. In response, the

United States would bomb targets within Iraq. Saddam would then mount an effective public relations campaign throughout the Arab world, showcasing U.S. brutality and Iraqi civilian casualties.

As part of the cease-fire agreed to in UN Security Council Resolution 687, Saddam was required to destroy SCUD missiles with a range greater than 150 kilometers. To enforce this requirement, the UN wanted to dispatch security inspectors to Iraq to verify that Saddam had indeed destroyed these weapons. Saddam also turned to the creation of weapons of mass destruction (WMD) to menace his neighbors with. These weapons programs would be a major justification for the 2003 invasion and Gulf War II.

Saddam did everything in his power to avoid or defeat the UN inspections, much to the consternation and frustration of the West. He frequently threatened to reinvade Kuwait and massed troops along the Kuwaiti border whenever the UN inspections got too onerous for Iraq. The UN Special Commission (UNSCOM) and the International Atomic Energy Agency were charged with overseeing Iraqi inspections. From the beginning, Saddam challenged them at every turn.

When the UNSCOM inspectors found evidence of Iraqi biological weapons programs, Saddam denied them access to their helicopters. He backed down after the United States and the UN interceded on the UNSCOM inspectors' behalf. In May 1992, Saddam admitted that Iraq was developing biological weapons. Later, UNSCOM discovered and began destroying chemical weapons. Saddam did everything he could to hide, obscure, and conceal the weapons programs and negotiated to lift the UN sanctions on his weapons and missiles.

In August 1995, two of Saddam's sons-in-law fled to Jordan, where they were granted asylum. The al-Majid brothers revealed Saddam's secrets, forcing Saddam to admit his illegal weapons programs, specifically the development of the deadly nerve agent VX. Saddam also revealed that Iraq was working on developing a nuclear weapon. Inexplicably, the al-Majid brothers voluntarily returned to Iraq six months later, and Saddam promptly had them executed.

Although the UNSCOM inspectors did destroy at least one of Saddam's chemical weapons plants in 1996, there was little doubt that Saddam continued breaching the terms of the cease-fire. Saddam gambled, correctly as it turned out, that the world would not take the necessary steps (military action) to stop him from developing

WMD or nuclear capabilities. The Western world continued bombing strikes and air raids while the Arab countries began to resent
what they perceived as unjust further Western interference in the
Arab world.

Despite continued bombing raids and repeated UN resolutions,
Saddam continued his cat-and-mouse games with the UNSCOM
inspectors. By 1998, he refused to allow any further weapons
inspections until the UN-imposed economic sanctions were lifted.
As we will see, Saddam waged a very effective public relations
campaign showcasing the devastating effects of the economic
sanctions.

The Clinton administration and Great Britain began Operation
Desert Fox in retaliation for Saddam's refusal to allow entry to the
UNSCOM weapons inspectors. These precision bombing strikes did
little to temper Saddam's belligerence. The UN ruled that UNSCOM
would now be known as the UN Monitoring, Verification, and
Inspection Commission (UNMOVIC) and that, if Saddam allowed
an additional nine months of weapons inspections, the UN would
lift all economic sanctions against Iraq. Saddam refused, and the
matter reached a stalemate until the second Bush administration
took action after the attacks of September 11, 2001.

In addition to requiring weapons inspections, the UN also instituted economic sanctions against Iraq at the close of Gulf War I.
The stated purpose of the sanctions was to support rebuilding
and reconstruction in Kuwait and to prevent Saddam from recon-
stituting his armies. Over the years, the sanctions lost much of
their luster in the eyes of the West because of Saddam's effective
public relations campaign. He showcased the devastating effects
of the sanctions on Iraqi citizens, especially Iraqi children. The
UN sanctions caused food shortages and health crises throughout
Iraq. Saddam made sure that his opposition—the Kurds and the
Shiites—suffered grievously under these sanctions.

In 1995, the UN created an oil-for-food program that would
allow Iraq to export oil as long as the revenue went toward the
purchase of food, medicine, and other needed supplies for the Iraqi
people. Initially, the UN, backed by the United States, demanded
some oversight into how the humanitarian aid was distributed so
that Saddam would not be able to oppress the Shiites and Kurds
through starvation and lack of access to medicine. Saddam stood
fast against this provision and eventually won. It should surprise
no one that the Sunnis received most of the humanitarian aid,

while the Shiites and the Kurds continued to suffer under the devastating effects of the sanctions.

Once it became apparent that the economic sanctions were doing little to prevent Saddam from his aggressive, bellicose tactics, and frightful weapons programs, most of the world wanted to end the Iraqi sanctions. The United States alone continued to support the sanctions as a preventive measure but was becoming increasingly isolated in its determination to defeat Saddam.

GULF WAR II

After the September 11 attacks on the United States by al-Qaeda, the second Bush administration adopted a policy of preemptive strikes against any enemy of the United States and declared a global "war on terrorism." After pursuing al-Qaeda in Afghanistan, the United States demanded that Iraq comply with the UN Security Council resolutions and allow the weapons inspectors full access to the country. Saddam refused. The United States then worked to build a coalition against Iraq, similar to the Western–Arab coalition that defended Kuwait during Gulf War I.

The United States alleged that Saddam possessed WMD (as of this writing, no WMD have been found), was attempting to purchase fissile material to constitute a nuclear weapon, and possessed ties to al-Qaeda and therefore posed an imminent threat to the United States. The United States highlighted the appalling Iraqi human rights record, especially Saddam's use of chemical weapons against his own people. The neoconservatives of the Bush administration also sought to instill democracy in Iraq as a model for the remainder of the Middle East and the world.

Iraq continued to deny that it possessed WMD but continued to refuse to allow UN inspectors access to verify their claims. In September 2002, the United States pressed the UN to grant a resolution authorizing force against Iraq. In November 2002, the UN passed a resolution demanding that Iraq allow UN inspections to continue. The resolution contained a provision to allow the use of military force if Iraq did not comply. Saddam again refused as the United States and its allies began amassing along Iraq's borders and throughout the Persian Gulf.

In late November 2002, Saddam finally gave in and allowed the UN inspectors access to Iraq. The initial UN report added nothing new, and most of the international community wanted to allow the inspectors more time to complete additional inspections. However, the United States and Great Britain wanted to press forward to complete their desired regime change. On March 18, 2003, President George W. Bush gave Saddam Hussein a 48-hour deadline to abdicate and depart Iraq.

On March 19, 2003, the United States, in conjunction with Great Britain and a much smaller "coalition of the willing" than in 1991, launched Operation Iraqi Freedom. All told, about 270,000 coalition troops were assembled on the Iraqi front. Within three weeks, Saddam Hussein's regime collapsed, and the Iraqi military surrendered. On April 8, 2003, U.S. forces captured Baghdad and toppled a statue of Saddam Hussein, symbolically ending his regime.

After an initial "decapitation strike" at an underground Baghdad bunker where Saddam was believed to be hiding, the United States unleashed an aerial assault intended to create "shock and awe" among the Iraqis. By March 21, the ground war began, led by U.S. General Tommy Franks, as the aerial assault on Baghdad continued. The United States quickly took the crucial port of Umm Qasr, close to the Kuwaiti border, and moved to secure the oil wells in southern Iraq. The United States wanted to prevent Saddam from setting fire to the oil fields as he did to the Kuwaiti wells at the close of Gulf War I.

The Iraqis did present some resistance, especially at Basra and Nassiriya. The Fedayeen and the Republican Guard were especially fierce opponents of the United States. The desert terrain itself also stopped the U.S. invasion when a fierce sandstorm began during the second week of the war. The United States was also vulnerable to suicide attacks by Arab "martyrs." Private Jessica Lynch became a household name when the reporters embedded with military units in Iraq reported her rescue from an Iraqi hospital.

As U.S. forces approached the capital, Saddam made use of human shields, suicide attacks, and urban street fighting to prevent the capture of the Iraqi capital. His information minister launched a bizarre disinformation campaign denying that U.S. troops were even in the country even though they could clearly be seen on the streets of the city. American troops first took the airport and renamed it Baghdad International. From that strategic base, they were able to take the city itself.

Although they were not able to capture the Iraqi dictator himself, they did topple a great statue of him to the cheering of Iraqi crowds. The U.S.-led coalition was shown relaxing in the opulent Iraqi presidential palaces and destroying the omnipresent portraits of Saddam. By April 9, 2003, the regime of Saddam Hussein had fallen.

IRAQ AFTER SADDAM HUSSEIN

To the great surprise of the United States, the Iraqis did not greet the Americans as liberators but instead perceived yet another Western-imposed dominion over Iraq. While many Iraqis are grateful that the dictator Saddam Hussein is gone, they fear and resent the continued U.S. presence in Iraq. The Sunnis, centered in the Sunni triangle, have especially resisted American forces. Although most of the Iraqi populace works peacefully with the American forces, the Iraqi insurgency has caused devastating western casualties and created considerable difficulty for those trying to secure the country.

The U.S.-led coalition was not able to prevent widespread looting and rampages throughout Iraqi after its swift victory. Antiquities such as the priceless Vase of Warka were taken from the National Museum (though later returned), and the National Library was destroyed. Additionally, the rampaging crowds devastated Iraqi infrastructure, already ravaged by 20 years of war and sanctions.

The fall of Saddam caused a leadership vacuum throughout Iraq, and power struggles ensued. Exiles such as Ahmad Chalabi returned to the country to take control and build up a power base. Even today, Iraq risks dissolving into fragments along cultural, religious, and tribal lines.

Saddam's sons, Uday and Qusay, who helped their father terrorize his subjects for so long, were killed in a Mosul firefight with American forces in July 2003. On December 13, 2003, Saddam was captured near his hometown of Tikrit hiding in a "spider hole." He awaits trial for crimes against humanity in an Iraqi prison where he spends his days tending a palm tree and penning poetry.

In the spring of 2004, the American news program *60 Minutes* displayed shocking photos of American GI prison guards abusing and mocking the detainees they guarded at Abu Ghraib prison. The Bush administration claimed that these were the actions of rogue soldiers and not sanctioned by the U.S. government. Several of the perpetrators of the Abu Ghraib scandal are serving prison terms, others are undergoing military tribunals and trials in the United States, and President Bush apologized for their disgraceful actions. However, the disturbing and revolting images that poured out of Abu Ghraib incited the Iraqi insurgency to increase levels of violence against the U.S. occupation and increased the Arabic opposition to the U.S. coalition in Iraq.

The Iraqi insurgency intensified immediately before the January 2005 elections. The insurgency, comprised of remnants of Saddam's Republican Guard, disaffected Sunnis, and others who had lost power during the U.S. occupation, has caused more than 1,000 American deaths. Desperate to stop the spread of democracy in the Middle East, they threatened to kill anyone who participated in the elections and terrorized both the populace and the occupiers. The U.S. officially granted sovereignty back to the Iraqi government on June 30, 2004, but remained to assist the interim Iraqi government.

On January 30, 2005, the Iraqis held their first free elections in more than 50 years. Although many Sunnis abstained from voting, millions of Iraqi's risked their lives to vote, and their ink-stained index fingers (required to prevent double voting) became symbols of hope for democracy around the world. Iraq's new 275-member National Assembly named Ibrahim Jaasari as Prime Minister and Rowsch Shaways, Ahmad Chalabi, and Abid al-Mutlaq al-Jabburi as deputy prime ministers. The National Assembly will create a constitution and run another election to elect a permanent Iraqi government.

In a major power shift, the Shiites have gained majority power by winning nearly half of all Iraqi votes. They have promised to create a secular Iraqi government, with representation guaranteed for all. It remains to be seen if they are equal to the task of integrating Iraq's disparate elements into a cohesive national union. Additionally, they must develop a police force and military to suppress the insurgency that still batters Iraq, and they face the task of rebuilding a country devastated by two decades of war and sanctions.

Iraq's future is uncertain. The recent elections indicate that Iraq is taking its first fledgling steps toward democracy and a free way of life for all Iraqis. However, the bloody insurgency continues, and U.S. troops will remain in Iraq for an indefinite period. The cultural, religious, and tribal fissures that underlie Iraq still exist. It is unknown whether the Shiites, Sunnis, and Kurds will be able to work together to create a unified country or descend into the chaos of a civil war. The world will be watching as Iraq continues to write its history on the sands of the Middle Eastern desert.

Notable People in the History of Iraq

Al-Bakr, Ahmad (1914–1982). First Ba'athist president of Iraq from 1968 to 1979.

Al-Barzini, Mustafa (1903–1979). Leader of the Kurdish Democratic Party until 1979. He was the leader of the Iraqi Kurdish national movement.

al-Bitar, Salah al-Din (1912–1980). Cofounder (with Michel Aflaq) of the Ba'ath Party.

Al-Gailani Rashid Ali (1892–1965). Led a 1941 revolt to end British influence in Iraq and played a major part in the Revolution of 1958.

Al-Majid, Ali Hasan (1941–). Former governor of the Kurdish region of Iraq, dubbed "Chemical Ali" for his use of chemical weapons against the Kurds during the *anfals* of the late 1980s.

Al-Mansur/Abu Jaffar (712?–775). Abbasid caliph who built the city of Baghdad in 762.

Al-Rashid, Harm (786–809). Abbasid caliph who defeated the Byzantines ushered in Baghdad's golden age. Famously mentioned in the story collection *The Thousand and One Nights.*

Al-Shawwaf, Abd al-Wahhab (?–1959). Leader of the 1959 Mosul Revolt.

As-Said, Nuri (1888–1958). Army general who rose to become prime minister of Iraq during the reign of Ghazi I and Faisal II until he was assassinated during the Revolution of 1958.

Aflaq, Michael (1910–1989). Cofounder in 1944 (with Salah al-Din al-Bitar) and ideologue of the Ba'ath Party, a spiritual movement with the stated goals of unity, liberty and socialism for the Arab world. He was secretary-general of the Ba'ath Party until his death in 1989.

Alexander the Great (356 B.C.E.–323 B.C.E.). Macedonian general who captured Babylon in 331 B.C.E., ushering in the Macedonian era.

Arif, Abd ar-Rahman (1916–). Brother to Abd al-Rahman Arif who took over the Iraqi presidency on the death of his brother in 1966.

Arif, Abd as-Salam (1921–1966). Leader of the Free Officers movement and participated in the Revolution of 1958. Imprisoned by his coconspirator, Quasim. After the revolution, he aligned with the Ba'athists. After the 1963 Ba'athist revolution, he became the Iraqi president and commander in chief.

Bell, Gertrude (1868–1926). Archaeologist who served as a British intelligence officer during World War I and liaison to the rural tribes of Mesopotamia. After the war, she served as "Oriental Secretary" to the British government in Iraq. Dubbed the "Uncrowned Queen of Iraq" because of her close relationship to King Faisal I.

Bush, George H. W. (1924–). President of the United States and leader of the 1991 Western–Arab coalition that drove Saddam Hussein out of Kuwait during Gulf War I.

Bush, George W. (1946–). President of the United States and leader during the attacks of September 11, 2001, and Gulf War II.

Chalabi, Ahmed (1944–). Leader of the exile Iraq National Congress group and returned to Iraq after the U.S.-led fall of Saddam Hussein.

Churchill, Winston (1874–1965). As British colonial secretary, he served as chairman of the Conference of Cairo in 1921, which laid the foundation for the post–World War I Iraqi government. Named Faisal I as the first king of Iraq.

Cyrus Achaemenes (559 B.C.E.–530 B.C.E.). King of the Persians and the Medes who conquered Babylon in 539 B.C.E., ushering in the Mede and Persian occupation of Mesopotamia.

Faisal I (1885–1933). Sat on the throne during the British Mandate following World War I, the first Hashemite King of Iraq ruled from 1921 to 1933.

Ghazi I (1912–1939). Second king of Iraq's Hashemite dynasty who ruled from 1933 to 1939. He was anti-British and supported pan-Arabism and Arab nationalism.

Hammurabi (alt. Hammurapi) (1792–1750 B.C.E.). First ruler of a unified Babylonia who made Marduk the divinity of the Babylonian Empire, thus creating the first monotheistic state. Created the Code of Hammurabi, which is the foundation for modern law.

Hussein, Saddam (1937–). President of Iraq from 1979 until his ouster by the United States in 2003. Served as vice president of Iraq during the regime of al-Bakr. Currently awaiting trial for crimes against humanity.

Khomeini, Ayatollah Ruhollah (1900–1989). Learned Shiite cleric who overtook Iran in 1979 and converted its government to a theocracy. He was the leader of the Iranians during the eight-year Iran–Iraq War.

Lawrence, Thomas Edward (1888–1935). A British military intelligence officer who helped organize Iraqi tribes to assist the British during World War I. Subject of the film *Lawrence of Arabia.*

Midhat Pasha (1822–1883). Ottoman governor of Mesopotamia from 1869 to 1872 who introduced a revised legal system, an educational system, and Mesopotamia's first newspaper.

Prophet Muhammad (570–632). Founder of the Islamic faith, which introduced the revolutionary concepts of monotheism, an Arabic afterlife, and the five pillars of Islam.

Nebuchadrezzar II (605–562 B.C.E.). Leader of Babylon at the height of the Neo-Babylonian Empire. Successfully defeated the Assyrians. Destroyed Jerusalem in 586 B.C.E. and took the Jews into captivity. Created the Hanging Gardens of Babylon, one of the wonders of the ancient world, and built the defensive Median wall north of Babylon and the famed Ishtar gate.

Qassim, General Abduel Karim (1914–1963). Leader of the Free Officers movement and participated in the Iraqi Revolution of 1958. He ruled Iraq as prime minister until 1963 and aligned with the Iraqi Communist Party.

Sargon I (2302–2247 B.C.E.). Warrior king who united the southern kingdom of Sumer and his own northern Akkad kingdom, thus setting the stage for Babylonia to develop. The Sargon dynasty endured until 2108 B.C.E. His name literally means "True King," and he was the founder of the first Mesopotamian dynasty.

Shah Abbas (1587–1629). Last great Persian Safavid shah who challenged the Ottoman's control of Iraq in 1622.

Sultan Ahmet III (1703–1730). Dubbed the "Tulip King" because of his enchantment with the Dutch flower, he introduced the printing press to the Ottoman Empire, ushering in an age of learning and literacy.

Sultan Sulaiman the Magnificent (1520–1566). Ottoman sultan who conquered Baghdad in 1534, thus introducing Ottoman rule to Mesopotamia. He was famous for his law codes, which combined Islamic religious law and everyday legal issues.

Umayyad, Muawiya (?–680). The governor of Syria who became the first ruler of the first hereditary Islamic dynasty, the Umayyads.

Ur-Nammu (2112–2094 B.C.E.). Ushered in the third dynasty of Ur. Built the great ziggurat of Ur and developed the principle of legal compensation.

Urukagina (ca. 2400 B.C.E.). Sumerian king who first recognized individual rights of citizens, thus setting the stage for the Code of Hammurabi.

Glossary

Anfals (Kurdish):   term for the brutal campaign of genocide by the regime of Saddam Hussein against the Kurds in the late 1980s. Literally "spoils."

Awilum (Babylonian):   Literally "man" but likely used to denote "freeman" or "property owner" in the Old Babylonian period.

Ayatollah: Roughly akin to a bishop in the Catholic Church hierarchy, an ayatollah is a significant religious leader to the Shiite Muslims.

Ba'ath (Arabic):   Insurrection and rebirth.

Basij: Iranian fighters during the Iran–Iraq War who were a group of devout Shiites willing to be martyred in battle. Many of them children, they were often used in "human wave" assaults against their outnumbered Iraqi counterparts.

Caliph: Islamic religious leader (alternate spelling "khalifa").

Caravansaries: Resting places for caravans built at 25-mile intervals throughout the Ottoman Empire.

Chaldean Sea: Modern-day Persian Gulf.

Code of Hammurabi (Babylonian):   Basis of all modern law, it was an elaborate code of laws covering commercial, civil, and criminal sections.

Devshirme (Turkish):   A practice during the Ottoman Empire of compelling non-Muslim male children to serve as slaves to the sultan. Literally "gathering."

Dhimmis: Islamic word for non-Muslims.

Divan (Turkish):   Council of advisers and ministers to the Ottoman sultan.

Edduba (Sumerian):   School, literally "tablet house."

Egalish (Babylonian):   Temple of Marduk.

En (Sumerian):   Title meaning "the lord." Most likely the title given to priests in the Sumerian city-states.

Ensis (Sumerian):   Title roughly translated to "governor."

Entemenaki (Babylonian):   A vast ziggurat in Babylon thought to be the biblical Tower of Babel.

Enuma Elish (Babylonian):   Epic literary tale in which Marduk triumphs over the forces of chaos. May have inspired the Old Testament writers.

Fez: Small hat worn by Ottoman reformers in place of the traditional turban. Became a symbol of the Tanzimat reforms.

Grand Vizier (Turkish):   Chief adviser to the Ottoman sultan (alternate spelling "wazier").

Harem: Literally "private." The private area of an Islamic home where females lived.

Hegira: The migration of Muslims from Mecca to Medina during the time of the Prophet Muhammad.

IAEA: International Atomic Energy Agency. Responsible for UN-sponsored weapons inspections after Gulf War I with the UNSCOM.

ICP (Iraqi):   Iraqi Communist Party.

Imam: Leader of an Islamic mosque.

Inanna (Sumerian):   Goddess of love and war, Queen of Heaven.

Iraq (Aramaic):   Black, muddy land.

Janissaries (Turkish):   Special fighting force of the Ottoman sultan.

Khan (Turkish):   Leader over multiple Turkish tribes.

Kharijites: Islamic group that believes that true piety is the most important qualification for a Muslim religious leader.

Lugal (Sumerian):   Literally "the great man." Title roughly translating to "king."

Madrassa: Islamic boys' school where the Quran was the focus of the curriculum.

Mamluks (Islamic):   Non-Arab slaves.

Mandate: After the Conference of San Remo in April 1920, the terror ties of the defeated Ottomans and Germans were divided into zones to be administered by the victorious European allies.

Marduk: Divinity of the Babylonian Empire. Usually depicted as a horned dragon.

Mecca: Birthplace of the Prophet Muhammad and thus the holiest site in the Islamic faith, located in modern-day Saudi Arabia.

Mesopotamia (Greek):   Land between the rivers.

Mevlevi: Sufi whirling dervishes who twirl as they chant the names of God.

Mihrab: A decorated wall niche in a mosque that shows the direction of Mecca.

Misharum (Babylonian):   Legal edicts.

Mosque: Islamic site of worship.

Muftis: Islamic legal scholars, especially in Ottoman times.

Muhafazah (Arabic):   Provinces.

Mujtahids: Overseers of the Shiite community.

Mushkenum (Babylonian):   Literally "greet with a gesture of adoration." Means "royal dependent" and denotes a class of citizens lower than the Awilum in Babylonian society.

Nanna (Sumerian):   Moon god.

NCRC (Iraqi):   National Council of Revolutionary Command.

Pan-Arabism: Movement that supports freedom for all Arab people with the ultimate goal of a united Arab homeland.

Pasdaran: Iranian "republican guard."

Pasha (Turkish):   Ottoman governors, especially of conquered territories.

Quran: Islamic religious text believed to contain the final authoritative word of Allah as revealed the Prophet Muhammad (alternate spelling "Koran").

RCC (Iraqi):   Revolutionary Command Council.

SAIRI: Supreme Assembly for the Islamic Revolution in Iran. Formed to unite the many Shiite groups working toward promoting an Islamic regime in Iraq.

Satrap: Persian overseer of Babylon.

Sea of the Rising Sun: Modern-day Persian Gulf.

Sharia: Islamic law derived from the Quran.

Sharif: Honorific title given to descendants of the Prophet Muhammad.

Sheik: Arabic tribal leader (alternate spelling "shaykh").

Shiites: Sect of Islamic faith that believe that the caliph must be a member of Ali or Muhammad's family. Although the majority of the Iraqi population consist of Shiites, they are the minority in the Islamic world (alternate spelling "Shi'a").

Shura: Islamic participative council.

Sufi: Islamic sect that rejects worldly goods in pursuit of a simple life.

Sultan: Ottoman ruler.

Sunni: Islamic sect that believes that the caliphate should be elected by a popular vote. Although the Sunnis are the minority within Iraq, they are the majority of Muslims throughout the world.

Tanzimat: Ottoman reforms of the late 1700s and early 1800s to attempt to bring democratic government and the Industrial Revolution to the Ottoman Empire.

Tell (Arabic):   Derived from the Babylonian word "tillum," meaning "mound" or "hill."

Topkapi: Opulent palace of the Ottoman sultans in Istanbul.

UNMOVIC: UN Monitoring, Verification, and Inspection Commission. The new name given to the UNSCOM after Operation Desert Fox.

UNSCOM: UN Special Commission responsible for weapons inspections during the 1990s along with the IAEA.

Vilayets (Turkish):   Ottoman provinces.

Vizier (Turkish):   Adviser to the sultan (alternate spelling "wazier").

Wardum (Babylonian):   Slave.

WMD: Weapons of mass destruction, including chemical, biological, and nuclear weapons.

Young Turks: Members of the Committee and Union and Progress who desired democratic reforms during the Ottoman Empire, including a constitution and a parliament.

Ziggurat (Sumerian):   Literally "to build high." A stepped tower of several flat platforms built one on top of the other and crowned by a temple.

Bibliographic Essay

Although the scholarly texts relevant to Iraq are vast, the selections recommended herein are limited to easily available English texts. Article and journals have been omitted. The most comprehensive general overviews of Iraqi history are Phebe Marr, *The Modern History of Iraq* (Boulder, Colo.: Westview Press, 2004); Gilles Munier, *Iraq: An Illustrated History and Guide* (Northampton, Mass.: Interlink Publishing, 2004); John Miller, ed., *Inside Iraq: The History, the People and the Modern Conflicts of the World's Least Understood Land* (New York: Marlowe & Company, 2002); and Charles Tripp, *A History of Iraq* (Cambridge: Cambridge University Press, 2002). For an Arabic perspective, consult Geoff Simmons, *Iraq: From Sumer to Saddam* (New York: St. Martin's Press, 1994).

For readers interested in Mesopotamia during ancient times, see A. Leo Oppenheim, *Ancient Mesopotamia: Portrait of a Dead Civilization* (Chicago: University of Chicago Press, 1977); J. N. Postgate, *Early Mesopotamia: Society and Economy at the Dawn of History* (London: Routledge, 1992); Harriet Crawford, *Sumer and the Sumerians* (Cambridge: Cambridge University Press, 1991); Susan Pollack, *Ancient Mesopotamia: The Eden That Never Was* (Cambridge: Cambridge University Press, 1999); Jeremy Black and Anthony Green, *Gods, Demons and Symbols of Ancient Mesopotamia* (Austin: University of Texas Press, 1997); M. E. L. Mallowan, *Early Mesopotamia and Iran* (London: Thames and Hudson, 1965); Samuel Noah Kramer, *History Begins at Sumer: Twenty Seven "Firsts" in Man's Recorded History* (Garden City, N.Y.: Doubleday Anchor Books, 1959); Hans J. Nissen, *The Early History of the Ancient Near East 9000–2000 BCE* (Chicago: University of Chicago Press, 1983); and Samuel Noah Kramer, *The Sumerians: Their History, Culture and Character* (Chicago: University of Chicago Press, 1963).

On Babylon, consult Elaine Laudau, *The Babylonians* (Brookfield, Conn.: Millbrook Press, 1997); H. E. L. Mellersh, *Sumer and Babylon* (New York: Thomas Y. Crowell, 1965); H. W. F. Saggs, *Everyday Life in Babylonia and Assyria* (New York: GP Putnam's Sons, 1965); and Joan Oates, *Babylon* (London: Thames and Hudson, 1979).

Although there are few books that deal specifically with Mesopotamia during the Islamic conquest, the following provide excellent general historical information on the period: Seyyed Hossein Nasr, *Islam: Religion, History and Civilization* (New York: HarperCollins, 2003); Karen Armstrong, *A History of God* (New York: Knopf, 1993); Karen Armstrong, *Islam: A Short History* (New York: Random House, 2002); John Esposito, ed., *The Oxford History of Islam* (Oxford: Oxford University Press, 1999); and Ira M. Lapidus, *A History of Islamic Societies* (Cambridge: Cambridge University Press, 2002).

Like the reference works on the Islamic conquest, works dealing with the Ottoman Empire do not separately address the history of Mesopotamia. However, some sources on the Ottoman Empire include Andrew Wheatcroft, *The Ottomans* (London: Penguin, 1993); Jason Goodwin, *Lords of the Horizons: A History of the Ottoman Empire* (New York: Henry Holt, 1998); Lord Kinross, *The Ottoman Centuries: The Rise and Fall of the Turkish Empire* (New York: Morrow Quill, 1977); and Colin Imber, *The Ottoman Empire* (New York: Palgrave Macmillan, 2002).

For the modern era, including during the period of Saddam Hussein, refer to Christopher Catherwood, *Churchill's Folly: How Winston Churchill Created Modern Iraq* (New York: Carroll & Graf, 2004); Marion Farouk-Sluglett and Peter Sluglett, *Iraq since 1958: From*

Revolution to Dictatorship (London: I.B. Tauris, 1990); Robert A. Fernea and W. M. Rodger Louis, eds., *The Iraqi Revolution of 1958: The Old Social Classes Revisited* (London: I.B. Tauris, 1991); Dilip Hiro, *Iraq: In the Eye of the Storm* (New York: Thunder's Mouth Press, 2002); William Paul Roberts, *The Demonic Comedy: Some Detours in the Baghdad of Saddam Hussein* (New York: Farrar, Straus and Giroux, 1997); Samir al-Khalil, *Republic of Fear: The Inside Story of Saddam's Iraq* (New York: Pantheon Books, 1989); Simon Henderson, *Instant Empire: Saddam Hussein's Ambition for Iraq* (San Francisco: Mercury House, 1991); Efraim Karsh and Inari Rautsi, *Saddam Hussein: A Political Biography* (New York: Free Press, 1991); and Dilip Hiro, *The Longest War: The Iran-Iraq Military Conflict* (New York: Routledge, 1991).

For women's studies, read Nuha al-Radi, *Baghdad Diaries: A Woman's Chronicle of War and Exile* (New York: Vintage Books, 2003); Jean P. Sasson, *Mayada: Daughter of Iraq* (New York: Dutton, 2003); and Janet Wallach, *Extraordinary Life of Gertrude Bell, Adventurer, Advisor to Kings, Ally of Lawrence of Arabia* (New York: Random House, 1996).

For the Gulf wars, consult Anthony H. Cordesman, *The Iraq War: Strategy, Tactics and Military Lessons* (Westport, Conn.: Praeger, 2003); Jean P. Sasson, *The Rape of Kuwait: The True Stories of Iraqi Atrocities against a Civilian Population* (New York: Knightsbridge Publishing, 1991); Michael Kelly, *Martyr's Day: Chronicle of a Small War* (New York: Random House, 1993); John Keegan, *The Iraq War* (New York: Knopf, 2004); John Lee Anderson, *The Fall of Baghdad* (New York: Penguin 2004); Yossef Bodansky, *The Secret History of the Iraq War* (New York: HarperCollins, 2004); and Richard Engel, *A Fist in the Hornet's Nest: On the Ground in Baghdad Before, During and After the War* (New York: Hyperion, 2004).

For Iraq today, read Joseph Braude, *The New Iraq: Rebuilding the Country for Its People, the Middle East and the World* (New York: Basic Books, 2003); Sandra Mackey, *The Reckoning: Iraq and the Legacy of Saddam Hussein* (New York: Norton, 2003); Noah Feldman, *What We Owe Iraq: War and the Ethics of Nation Building* (Princeton, N.J.: Princeton University Press, 2004); Christine Bird, *A Thousand Sighs/A Thousand Revolts* (New York: Ballantine, 2004); Liam Anderson and Gareth Stansfield, *The Future of Iraq: Dictatorship, Democracy or Division?* (New York: Palgrave Macmillan, 2004); and Steven Strasser, *The Abu Ghraib Investigations* (New York: Public Affairs, 2004).

Index

About the Author

COURTNEY HUNT is an attorney for the federal government and a freelance writer.

Other Titles in the Greenwood Histories of the Modern Nations
Frank W. Thackeray and John E. Findling, Series Editors

The History of Argentina
Daniel K. Lewis

The History of Australia
Frank G. Clarke

The History of the Baltic
States
Kevin O'Connor

The History of Brazil
Robert M. Levine

The History of Canada
Scott W. See

The History of Chile
John L. Rector

The History of China
David C. Wright

The History of Congo
Didier Gondola

The History of Cuba
Clifford L. Staten

The History of Egypt
Glenn E. Perry

The History of France
W. Scott Haine

The History of Germany
Eleanor L. Turk

The History of Ghana
Roger S. Gocking

The History of Great Britain
Anne Baltz Rodrick

The History of Holland
Mark T. Hooker

The History of India
John McLeod

The History of Iran
Elton L. Daniel

The History of Ireland
Daniel Webster Hollis III

The History of Israel
Arnold Blumberg

The History of Italy
Charles L. Killinger

The History of Japan
Louis G. Perez

The History of Korea
Djun Kil Kim

The History of Mexico
Burton Kirkwood

The History of New
Zealand
Tom Brooking

The History of Nigeria
Toyin Falola

The History of Poland
M.B. Biskupski

The History of Portugal
James M. Anderson

The History of Russia
Charles E. Ziegler

The History of Serbia
John K. Cox

The History of South Africa
Roger B. Beck

The History of Spain
Peter Pierson

The History of Sweden
Byron J. Nordstrom

The History of Turkey
Douglas A. Howard